HOW TO SURVIVE IDENTITY THEFT

REGAIN YOUR MONEY, CREDIT, AND REPUTATION

DAVID H. HOLTZMAN
SECURITY CONSULTANT AND PRESIDENT OF GLOBALPOV.COM

Avon, Massachusetts

Published by Adams Business,
an imprint of Adams Media, a division of F+W Media, Inc.
57 Littlefield Street, Avon, MA 02322. U.S.A.
www.adamsmedia.com

ISBN 10: 1-60550-148-4
ISBN 13: 978-1-60550-148-2

Printed in the United States of America.

10 9 8 7 6 5 4 3 2 1

Library of Congress Cataloging-in-Publication Data
is available from the publisher.

This publication is designed to provide accurate and authoritative information with regard to the subject matter covered. It is sold with the understanding that the publisher is not engaged in rendering legal, accounting, or other professional advice. If legal advice or other expert assistance is required, the services of a competent professional person should be sought.

—From a *Declaration of Principles* jointly adopted by a Committee of the American Bar Association and a Committee of Publishers and Associations

Many of the designations used by manufacturers and sellers to distinguish their product are claimed as trademarks. Where those designations appear in this book and Adams Media was aware of a trademark claim, the designations have been printed with initial capital letters.

This book is available at quantity discounts for bulk purchases.
For information, please call 1-800-289-0963.

To my wonderful wife Tara
and my lovely grandchildren
Lilly, Will, and Jackson

Regard your good name as the richest jewel you can possibly be possessed of—for credit is like fire; when once you have kindled it you may easily preserve it, but if you once extinguish it, you will find it an arduous task to rekindle it again.

—Socrates

CONTENTS

PART I

IDENTITY CRIMES AND CRIMINALS

01.

YOUR IDENTITY CRISIS

Sarah Gonzalez was fuming in the checkout line at Macy's. The clerk had just informed her that her Visa card had been denied and she couldn't understand why. She'd always been meticulous about paying her bills on time, and this was especially true when it came to paying down her credit cards. She was planning to buy a house next year and was counting on her good credit score to obtain a favorable mortgage. The clerk handed her the telephone so that she could talk to the Visa security representative. She listened, stunned, as he told her that her $10,000 limit was maxed out. "I only had a few hundred dollars on my balance when I last got a bill," she protested. She began to cry.

Identity theft is the first truly new crime of the Information Age. Just as train robbery followed the invention of the steam engine, identity theft trailed right behind the development of our contemporary society and the revolutionary developments in computers, communications, big business, and big government that came with it.

DAMAGES

More than direct financial harm can result from identity theft. Identity problems will almost always end up causing havoc with your credit rating because, while the identity thief may take on almost every aspect of your financial life, he or she most assuredly won't pay your bills.

Thieves can and do steal income tax refunds, even ones based on falsely filed returns. They can intercept and cash any kind of government or corporate check, be it welfare, Social Security, food stamps, disability, pension, or insurance.

It doesn't have to be money either. It could be as insubstantial as frequent flyer miles or as solid as property. There have been cases where people have had cars and boats stolen and sold, and some victims have even had their houses and land taken from them.

All of the damages are not necessarily tangible. One of the most substantial and lasting consequences of identity theft is the damage done to your reputation. After your identity is snatched, the thief becomes you so that you are blamed for whatever they do. In this modern, computer-driven world, your credit report is your reputation.

As our lives become decentralized because of automated institutions, we no longer meet the people we do business with. Because of this, knowing your authentication secrets is sufficient proof to allow someone else to do anything that you can do. To identify ourselves to these strangers—since we don't know their faces or voices—we use machine-readable real-world identifiers such as name, address, and Social Security number, as well as synthesized ones like user IDs, account numbers, and passwords. These digital tags open the door to contemporary commerce, but they also open the door to identity theft.

THIS TIME IT'S PERSONAL

Identity theft is among the most personal of all crimes. If someone uncovers enough of your personal information, they can pretend to be you. Then they can use your identity to take the things that belong to you—your money, your tax refunds, your credit score and cards, your insurance benefits, or your car.

Our desire for convenience makes the situation worse. While forcing everyone to go into a bank, show two forms of identification, and get fingerprinted might not completely eliminate identity theft, there's no question we'd be a lot safer. Unfortunately, this sort of thing is not convenient. We want to bank by phone or over the Internet.

All this adds up to relative safety for a thief when he or she tries to pass for you online, as compared to say, forging one of your checks and trying to cash it in a liquor store.

What kind of data does an identity thief steal? Some are public knowledge, like your name, address, phone number, and birthday. Some are semi-private, such as your employer, previous addresses, work history, educational background, and family members. Some information is private but not hard to find, like your Social Security (SSN), cell phone, or driver's license number. Some data are more difficult to get but worth the effort because of the potential payoff for a thief. In general, the more secret the information a dishonest person is able to steal from you, the greater their reward—and the greater your loss.

Very private information might include the numbers of your bank accounts, credit card numbers, user IDs, or your passwords. Possession of these allows the thief direct access to money in your existing accounts without having to go through the hassle of opening up new ones. On the other hand, Federal Trade Commission (FTC) statistics indicate that opening up new accounts in the victim's name is the most lucrative for thieves and the most difficult for the victim to deal with.

Identity theft threatens each of us, every day. Every time we hand a waiter our credit card, throw a bank statement into the trash can instead of shredding it, or let our antivirus protection on our home computer lapse, we expose ourselves to a little bit more risk. Chances are that sooner or later someone somewhere will take advantage of that carelessness.

YOUR PERSONAL IDENTIFYING INFORMATION IS EASY TO GET

The basic problem, of course, is that it's not too difficult for others to tap into your personal information. Once someone has your name, address, birth date, driver's license, and some simple family information, he or she can successfully masquerade as you. As far as most of the companies that you do business with are concerned, this person might as well be you! With the addition of some financial information like an account number, an identity thief can conduct transactions, sell your assets, withdraw your money, or open up new credit accounts in your name.

Once someone gets a little of your identifying information, such as your Social Security or driver's license number, they can easily get past most identity challenge systems and access your accounts. Driver's license numbers are a matter of public record in many states and are even sold in bulk by several. These states make money by packaging a group of their residents' driving records, often including Department of Motor Vehicles (DMV) photos.

Social Security numbers, unfortunately, exist in far too many databases, both public and private, to remain secret very long. Many cell phone providers use them as account numbers and almost half of all U.S. universities and colleges still use the SSN as a student ID number. In the past, some states used them on driver's licenses, and some financial institutions used them as account numbers. (The former is now illegal, the latter actively discouraged.)

Think about how many times you've been asked for your Social Security number. All credit reports have them. Most government agencies identify you by your Social Security number, so that it's included in all kinds of government files and documents.

Companies are using creative new authentication schemes that use less-traditional information, such as asking trivia questions that only you would know. Sometimes you give them these answers when you get a user ID, but some companies discover them independently by hiring third party database vendors to "data-mine" information on you. The problem with these schemes is that they're just temporarily addressing the problem; eventually the answers to these questions will also end up in someone's database and they will be rendered useless as effective challenge questions. Celebrities are especially prone to this kind of attack because so much of their private life is publicized, and this is probably why so many of them get their identity stolen.

GRIM STATISTICS

Identity theft has grown into a major problem for businesses and consumers alike. The definitive survey of identity theft in this country was commissioned by the FTC in 2003, with a follow-up study in 2005. According to the original report, 12.7 percent of those surveyed said that their personal information had been misused within the previous five years, and 4.6 percent claimed to be victims of identity theft in the year the survey was conducted. That means that nearly 10 million people had their identity stolen in just that one year. The agency estimated that consumers and businesses lost nearly $53 billion to identity theft during that year.

The survey found that the median value of goods and services obtained by identity thieves in 2005 was $500. Ten percent of thieves acquired $6,000, while five percent took a median $13,000. We can see from this that most identity thefts are not that financially damaging, but a few cases are disproportionately harmful. It should also be remembered that many of the thieves probably attacked hundreds, even thousands of victims at a time. Identity theft is very lucrative for those who practice it on a large scale.

The figures showing how difficult it can be to repair the damage can be more important to victims. Ten percent spent fifty-five hours to rebuild the integrity of their personal information, while five percent needed 130 hours.

These statistics illustrate that identity theft is here to stay. As long as electronic record keeping, online communication, and online purchasing continue to be central to our lives, we can expect that thieves will try to use these conveniences as tools to steal from us.

HOW DID MY IDENTITY GET STOLEN?

A digital identity is primarily numbers—Social Security, telephone, weight, height, age, and birth date. In the modern world, we don't often have direct contact with the people we do business with, so we need secure ways to be identified. The easiest method is to see whether we correctly know personal identifiers like Social Security, telephone, or account numbers, or shared secrets like passwords. Sometimes trivia from our life like our first pet's name, elementary school, or mother's maiden name might be asked. And public information like our address or employer can be used as a secondary check.

This kind of database-driven verification works well no matter where the parties are located. At a time when companies have call centers from Ireland to India, headquarters around the country, and customers across the globe, this sort of identification is ideal. The person on the other end of the phone will never meet you. He just needs to ask you a question and compare your answer to the information on his screen.

It even works without a person. Challenge questions can be automatically constructed from information stored in a database and used for granting access to sensitive websites like credit card or telephone account management systems. Automated systems can even be run from telephones; voice recognition has gotten quite good in the last few years.

There are four sections in this book:

- The first is *descriptive*—an introduction to the post-modern crime of identity theft.
- The second is *prescriptive*—how to survive identity theft when it's happened to you.
- The third section is *defensive*—how to avoid getting your identity stolen in the first place.
- The fourth section contains resources to help you with identity theft problems, either before or after the theft has occurred.

If you're reading this book, in all likelihood you've suffered from identity theft. You're probably hurt, confused, angry, and vulnerable, very much the emotions Sarah Gonzalez felt as she stood weeping into the phone at Macy's. But you need to fight back the tears, and get ready to put your life back together. In this book, you'll discover the tools and resources you need to reclaim your credit and your reputation. And you'll know better how to prevent this sort of thing from ever happening to you again.

There are many different ways to steal personal information. Some of them are modern versions of well-established con games; some require vast resources and technological expertise. Most of the damage, though, is done by simple thievery—so simple that it's hard to believe it's so effective. Let's look at a few of the quick and easy ways the identity thieves gain access to your personal information.

02.

PETTY THIEVERY—
AND HOW TO AVOID IT

Despite the media's emphasis on computer hackers, your identity is more likely to be compromised by a physical theft than by an online hack. There are far too many places in the real world that contain personal information; places like wallets, purses, or mailboxes. Some thieves look for crumpled up credit card receipts outside stores and restaurants; others are institutional garbage pickers or "dumpster divers" who make a living out of finding valuable identification in your trash.

The typical identity thief is more likely to be an expert at the "social con" than a young, nerdy computer hacker. Many are very personable smooth talkers. They have to be because, sooner or later, they will have to pick up the phone and try to trick someone into giving them more information. Whether they talk someone at the phone company into giving them access to your account, or sweet-talk your health insurance information out of your doctor's office, they rely on the fact that Americans in general are trusting, helpful people who love to share information.

Not all of the thieves depend on charm, however. Many depend on our laziness, our love of convenience, or our ignorance of even simple security measures. Here are a few examples of how simple it can be to steal your identity.

OPPORTUNISTS

Randy pushed his janitorial cart between the desks, stopping to empty the wastebaskets and throw away obvious trash. Every once in a while, he'd check over his shoulder nervously and pull out the writing shelf on one of the desks. At 2:30 in the morning, after having tried the same thing at dozens of desks throughout the building, he struck pay dirt just outside an executive VP's office. There was a long list of passwords—to important-sounding systems—taped to a desk drawer. Randy hurriedly copied them down on a memo pad that he carried with him for just this purpose. Pleased with his night's work, he started planning how he'd spend the money he'd get for the list.

Many identity thefts are not the products of crime syndicates or even dedicated professionals. They are, instead, the actions of opportunists.

Like the citizen walking down the street who decides to keep the cash from a wallet found on the sidewalk, the impulsive identity thief does not act out of premeditation. She may never have considered herself capable of stealing. Yet, when presented with what appears to be a low-risk chance to make some money, she takes advantage of the circumstances.

These circumstances could include a password carelessly taped to a desk drawer at work or a pre-approved credit card offer addressed to a neighbor that is inadvertently delivered to the wrong address. Perhaps some credit cards dropped in a hotel hallway, or some paperwork left in a car dropped off at a repair shop present the opportunity that could lead to identity theft.

Regardless of how it happens, the motivation of the thief is always the same—easy money. He or she may not have a criminal background, but they are quick to see a chance to make some easy cash.

This basic human weakness is the reason we need to lock our doors, update our passwords, and guard our account numbers. It's unlikely that a professional thief will search your desk at work or a criminal gang will ransack your hotel room, but by keeping your valuable personal information secure and out of sight, you can avoid creating an irresistible temptation for the *amateur* identity thief.

LONE WOLVES

Terry Shannon started the morning the way he did every Tuesday, by poking through the dumpsters behind the airport hotels, looking for credit card receipts. He had a particularly rewarding morning, finding twelve at the Marriott alone. After a latte and a break, he stopped at the local computer repair shop to visit his "friend" Sid.

Sid nodded when he came into the store and handed him a homemade CD. Terry surreptitiously slipped him a hundred dollar bill in return. He'd work his way through the information stolen from customers' computers over the weekend, adding the names, addresses, and bank account information to the spreadsheet he called his "Victims" list.

That afternoon, back at his apartment, he went shopping online for some new clothes and an emerald ring for his girlfriend's birthday. He had the purchases shipped to another "friend's" apartment. Terry paid $800 per month for this privilege. He had never run a big con, but he was a professional identity thief, making close to $100,000 a year, mostly by credit card scamming. He reported the income on his taxes—under a phony business name—because he didn't want to cause any trouble with the IRS. After all, that's how Al Capone got caught!

A few individual crooks use computers to get what they want, but they tend to be amateurs, not computer experts. They are, in the lingo, "script kiddies," using freely available software developed by real hackers.

Most want something more easily convertible into cash. They need to make a living from their efforts and are primarily interested in credit cards and bank accounts. They are the masters of the quick kill and don't have time for large-scale scams that take weeks or months to perpetrate. This class of criminal usually spends a lot of time on the run, moving from location to location, setting up temporary mail drops and buying "burners"—pay-as-you-go cell phones—from convenience stores; anything that makes their operations harder to track.

Howie Myers nodded his head in time with the mariachi music as he waited for the server to ring up his credit card. He had been in Tijuana all day and had been using his credit card liberally, but usually it was returned right away—like they did in the States. After twenty minutes, the surly waiter returned and dropped his card and the signature slip onto the table. Howie looked at his card uneasily. It occurred to him how easy it would have been for the waiter to make a copy. He determined that he would pull a copy of his credit report in a couple of weeks and make sure that everything was still okay. He carefully folded the receipt and put it away in his wallet.

Some identity thieves are experts at using credit card skimmers or at making arrangements with store clerks or restaurant staff to harvest customer credit card numbers.

Some of these professionals specialize in dumpster diving. They haunt residential neighborhoods or office buildings right before garbage pickups so that they can poke through the paper refuse looking for personal information or, even better, login IDs and passwords for online accounts.

This is an easy and relatively risk-free way to get personal information from individuals or system passwords from businesses. Most people, whether at home or at work, do not adequately destroy their sensitive information. Unless you burn it or run it through a cross-cut shredder, a determined hacker can usually get something out of your paper documents, even if he has to brush aside the coffee grinds to do so.

It's also common to read about privacy disclosures caused by corporate sloppiness. For example, one newspaper publisher wrapped stacks of its papers in printouts of customer credit card numbers! You almost couldn't design a better—or less traceable—way of giving away sensitive information.

Another simple form of identity theft is cashing in pre-approved credit card offers sent to the wrong address. A lot of people have old or incorrect addresses still listed on their credit reports. As a result, credit card companies will mail pre-approved offers to the right person but at a wrong address. By simply forging a signature and figuring out the answers to one or two relatively simple questions, an opportunistic identity thief can get a brand new credit card with your name on it and your good credit behind it.

But it doesn't always take an obviously sensitive piece of paper, like a pre-approved credit card offer, to get you into trouble. Most of us "archive" reams of sensitive personal information—including credit card and bank statements, mortgage applications, receipts that show credit card numbers, etc.—that we move between file cabinets and cellars and closets. What happens when you need to clean out your old files? How secure are they during a move, or when you're having your carpets cleaned?

INFORMATION BROKERS AND CUSTOMER SERVICE

Other thieves are middlemen, making a nice secondary income by selling lists of account information stolen from work computers. There have been many insider cases like these involving stock brokerages, credit card processors, direct marketers, and even government employees.

There are also many well-documented cases of computer repair techs stealing information from the machines they work on. Letting a knowledgeable person have access to your computer is like giving them the combination to your wall safe and leaving the house for the rest of the day. Some of these technicians see a customer's computer as an irresistible temptation—an opportunity for a no-risk scavenger hunt for porn, games, or other valuables. They won't take anything—that you'll notice—but they might make copies of your financial statements, banking files, or, even worse, password lists. With these in hand they're able to directly access your financial accounts, and might be able to withdraw, spend, or transfer your money.

If your identity hasn't been snagged by one of these simple techniques, it's only because there is a wealth of sensitive information in the world and not enough identity thieves to get around to it all. To make matters worse, this kind of crime is relatively inefficient compared to the more sophisticated, larger-scale scams that are also after your identity. We'll take a look at some of those in the following two chapters. In the meantime, chapter 10 offers a quick list of preventive measures you can take to limit your exposure.

03.

SPAMS AND SCAMS— AND HOW TO RECOGNIZE THEM

The worst identity thieves are not individuals practicing simple scams like those in the previous chapters, but rather large, organized rings; many located in Eastern Europe or Africa. They have turned identity theft into a big business worth many tens of millions of dollars per year. Some countries have become havens for identity thieves the way Somalia has built high sea piracy into a national moneymaker. For example, Nigeria is to identity theft what Florida is to oranges.

Unlike individual thieves, these gangs frequently have sophisticated technical expertise. They engineer custom viruses (like 2009's Conficker virus) specifically designed to overpower individual computers and either extract financial information from the hard drive or transform the victimized computer into a "zombie," a computer that a hacker has taken over that can be used later to attack a better-defended, higher-profile target. Gangs are interested in operations that can target thousands or even millions of people at a time. They are willing to play the numbers, using rigged e-mails or websites to catch a few people, here or there, who accidentally stray into their online traps. By tinkering with a few details, a gang can run the same con over and over again for years.

Since they are often located in countries with governments apathetic about online fraud, they are hard to stop even when detected by American legal authorities.

Ultimately, of course, they too need to extract money from their victims. It's at this point that they can be caught. Eventually, they need to show up at an Automatic Teller Machine (ATM) or a bank or present a phony credit card at a store or a phony passport at an airport. Like counterfeiters, their biggest exposure comes at the moment of truth when they try to get paid.

PHISHING FOR DOLLARS

Carol Tran felt like an idiot as she waited on hold on the phone for the bank security people to take her call. She'd gotten a piece of e-mail this morning from Citibank that said that someone had been using her account and that she had to change her password.

She'd never been too comfortable with the Internet anyway. Banking online seemed risky. When she clicked the link in the e-mail to bring up the Citibank site, she was asked to put in her old password and user ID. Then the link prompted her to type in a new password. She noted approvingly that they made her retype the new password so that she didn't mistype something and get locked out of her account.

Hours later, her good mood had evaporated. She'd mentioned the incident to her daughter, who told her that the website might have been fake and that she might have just given her password to identity thieves. Quickly, she tried to log back into her banking account only to find neither her new nor her old password worked. She picked up the phone and called Citibank.

Many of the unwanted e-mails, called spam, on your computer are actually thinly disguised attempts to get at your personal information. One popular form of this is called "phishing"; a con artist sends you (and probably hundreds if not thousands of others) an e-mail that apparently comes from a reputable business. If she's lucky, and you're not, it's from a company that you already have a relationship with; a bank, or an Internet site like E*TRADE, eBay, or Amazon.

The con artist wants to convince you to type in your personal and, hopefully, financial account information. Her e-mail:

- Looks, and reads, like a perfectly normal communication from a legitimate business
- May include the business's logo, its (real) address and phone number, and even its legal disclaimers
- Will contain a perfectly reasonable-sounding explanation for why you should click on an authentic-looking link to the company's website and log into your account

For example, it may say there's a problem with your account that needs to be fixed. It may even make you a special offer on goods or services. Unfortunately, it's easy to copy a legitimate website's pages just by writing a little software (this is also known as "spoofing"). The phony link included in the phony e-mail points to an equally phony website that looks just as authentic and trustworthy as the e-mail, but which is controlled by the con artist. Once you type your account ID and your password into the phony web page, your online identity belongs to the con artist.

To give you an idea of what to look out for in your e-mail, a few quick examples of phishing at work appear on the following pages. The first one is right to the point: It claims that your eBay account has been suspended and you need to click on the link to verify your credit card information. Once you get to the fake website, the scammers will attempt to squeeze whatever information that they can from you— address, Social Security number, birth date, account numbers, etc.

> Dear Sir or Madam,
>
> eBay Account Management regrets to inform you that your eBay account has been suspended due to credit card verification problems. Your credit card failed to authorize and, as a result, your account has been flagged. All further transactions with your account will be denied until this flag is removed.
>
> Please take a moment to confirm your account by going to the following address: eBay.com
>
> Truly yours, eBay account management team.

The trick, of course, is that the "eBay.com" link in the e-mail doesn't really take you to eBay.com. The scammer has coded the e-mail to show "eBay.com" while the link actually points elsewhere. Most browsers and e-mail programs let you look at the actual address of the link. If you check, you'll probably find that it leads to something like "eBayy.com" or even something unreadable like "xzzxzzxx.cn."

The next e-mail, pretending to be from Google AdWords, is more elaborate. If you happened to run a website that used Google AdWords, you might believe it enough to click on the link. The link is not really to Google, of course, but to a phishing site. The con artists behind it are trying to harvest your credit card numbers.

> Dear Google AdWords Customer,
>
> Your ads have stopped running because we were unable to process your billing information. We will reactivate your account after you update your billing information. In order to reactivate your account, please sign into your account at adwords.google.com—log in, and update your billing information. Once your account is reactivated and your billing information has been processed, your ads and campaigns can begin running immediately on Google.

You will not be asked to submit your billing information every time you create a new ad or campaign. If your payment has been declined and you'd like to resubmit the same credit card information, you may also do so by clicking the Retry card button on your Billing Preferences page. After updating your credit card information (regardless of whether or not you use a different card), it can take up to twenty-four hours before your ads start running again. You also have the option of providing a backup credit card to help ensure that your ads run continuously in the case that your primary payment method fails.

Sincerely,

The Google AdWords Team

Another phishing note, aimed at PayPal users, is more interesting because of the way they hide the actual Internet address of the link. Notice the hexadecimal TCP/IP address in the link below, disguising the actual address.

We recently reviewed your account, and we need more information about your business to allow us to provide uninterrupted service. Until we can collect this information, your access to sensitive account features will be limited. We would like to restore your access as soon as possible. We apologize for the inconvenience.

Why is my account access limited?

Your account access has been limited for the following reason(s):

We have reason to believe that your account was accessed by a third party. Because protecting the security of your account is our primary concern, we have limited access to sensitive

> PayPal account features. We understand that this may be an inconvenience but please understand that this temporary limitation is for your protection.
>
> Your case ID for this reason is PP-136-124-102.
>
> How can I restore my account access?
>
> Please visit the Resolution Center (0x3d2f3b05—) <http://0x3d2f3b05/www.paypal.com/cgi-bin/webscr/cmd=_login-run/)> and complete the steps described to remove any limitations.
>
> Completing all of the checklist items will automatically restore your account access.

Like the others, of course, this is not a legitimate PayPal site, and if you do type in your information it will go directly to the con artists.

Banks and credit card companies know full well that there are thousands of similar e-mails in circulation pretending to be from their companies. They also know that if they send an e-mail that looks like this kind of spam, many (rightly) suspicious people will disregard it. If you're ever in doubt that the message you see is real, you can always go directly to the company's website by typing in the URL yourself instead of clicking on the (insecure) link. If you really want to be safe, though, you should call the company directly.

SPEAR PHISHING AND OTHER VARIATIONS ON A THEME

Jeremy Gill was pleased to be honored with a special award. He'd gotten an e-mail this morning from an international selections agency that named him for a special *Who's Who* mention. They had obviously done their homework because they knew that he went to Harvard, that he lived in Brooklyn, and even which firm he was currently working at. Clearly they were on the up-and-up and it was about time that he got some recognition. Jeremy typed in his American Express number so he could preorder a copy of the 2009 *Who's Who* he'd be featured in. He also put in his Social Security number to validate his identity so the publishers could be sure it was him.

Just after he hit "send" he was assailed by doubts. He called a friend, who advised him to cancel his credit card immediately. As he punched in the telephone number for American Express, he berated himself. How could he have fallen for something so obvious?

Spear phishing is a variation of phishing that is rare today, but will probably become commonplace in the near future. Phishing is a numbers game; send out millions of notes and statistically some of the recipients will have an account with the spoofed financial institution and be gullible enough to fall for the scam. Spear phishing, on the other hand, is a more targeted approach (hence the pointed prefix "spear"). Spear phishers have done their homework and already know something about you. A note from a spear phisher might mention one of your friends by name, or maybe your mother. It might contain your Social Security Number or allude to an old job or address. A good spear phish note will look real; as though it comes from someone that you know.

There's even a new subcategory of spear phishing, called "whaling," which targets celebrities or known wealthy people.

In the meantime you'll have to depend on the old, if inexact, adage: "If it's too good to be true, it probably is."

PRETEXTING

As with most contemporary online scams, phishing and spear phishing have their "analog" precedents. As hard as it may be to believe, it's not that difficult to get your personal information over the telephone—from a service company, for example. Cell phone companies, for instance, generally use simple "challenge questions," such as providing the last 4 digits of your Social Security number along with your billing address. As we've seen, though, SSNs and billing addresses are not that hard to discover. Once a potential thief makes it through this security challenge, he has full access to your account and can change the Personal Identification Number (PIN) or password, or reset your mailing address or account information.

In one well-publicized case in 2006, the chairperson of Hewlett-Packard used a team of investigators to find out who had been leaking sensitive corporate information to the press. Among other techniques, the investigators used pretexting to gain access to the phone records of several of HP's board members as well as nine journalists, including reporters for *CNET*, *The New York Times*, and *The Wall Street Journal*.

OLD-FASHIONED HIGH-TECH SCAMMERS

There's another kind of online spam that can also be dangerous and closely resembles traditional scams. Instead of simply trying to steal your account information, they try to involve you in an elaborate and time-consuming con game.

The most notorious of these are the Nigerian e-mails. (They're called "Nigerian" e-mails because many of them originate from Nigeria, although no one country has a monopoly on creative Internet fraud.) The e-mails are variations of a 150-year-old con called the Spanish Prisoner. It goes like this: Someone with an official-sounding title contacts you by e-mail. He asks you to help him "launder" (illegally transfer) a huge amount of money out of Nigeria. He will deposit the entire huge amount of money into your account, and then arrange a way to pick up a large part of the huge amount later. For your time and trouble and secrecy you will get to keep the rest of the huge amount for yourself. Sounds pretty compelling, right? And pretty profitable! The only thing that you have to do is send him the account information for your bank, so he can wire you the money. Sounds too good to be true, right?

Well, it is. Maybe it would help to ask yourself a few pertinent questions like: "Why would the Nigerian Minister of Oil want to send me $50 million?" The Nigerian notes are also notorious for their poor spelling and grammar. You might wonder why the head of security for Chase Manhattan Bank in New York does not enjoy a mastery of the English language.

If any e-mail leaves you in doubt about the sender's authenticity, you're probably right. Trust your instincts. Even if the language and grammar are perfectly crafted, however, any offer to send you $50 million is probably suspect, and more than likely part of an effort to separate you from your bank account information.

Here is a good example of one of the infamous Nigerian letters. Look at misspelled words like *Contarct*, *Monetory*, *Cotract* and *ellected*.

> From: Mr. Hackey John
>
> I am a Diplomat from Nigeria to United Kingdom named Hackey John, mandated to deliver your Contarct/Inheritance sum to you in your country of residence.
>
> The funds total US$50 Million and you were made the beneficiary of these funds by our Ministry (F.G.N with U.K Monetory Regulation Banks Agency); after long time delay of your Cotract/Inheritance payment the new ellected Government and prime-Minister agreed to pay all outstanding payment of Inheritance/contractors which your name was among those that will be paid through diplomatic means.
>
> Sir, please re-confirm your cotract detials to enable me proceed to you address as I am presently at JFK Airport in the United States of America and before I can deliver the funds to you, you have to reconfirm the following information so as to ensure that I am dealing with the right person:

1. Full Name
2. Residential Address
3. Age
4. Occupation
5. Direct Telephone Numbers
6. Contract Number

After verification of the information with what I have on file, I shall contact you so that we can make arrangements on the exact time I will be bringing your package Consignment to your residential address. Send the requested information so that we can proceed.

Regards,

Hackey John

Here's another example of a scam e-mail. It's a simple request for your personal information from a well-known company. The note appeals to your greed by offering you the relatively modest sum (for e-mail scams) of half a million pounds. Notice the telltale giveaways: the misspellings of words like *Britain* and *retrieved* and the grammatical mistakes similar to those commonly made by a non-native speaker such as "in respect of your parcel," "Before the delivery protocols commenced," and "without any further hesitations." (The end of the e-mail, which I've deleted here, is a request for details of the recipient's account information.)

Good day.

This is the FedEx courier service company mailing you in respect of your parcel that we have in our office to be delivered to you. Before the delivery protocols commenced, there was a misunderstanding between you and the National Insurance Corporation in London over the Insurance Certificate which caused the delay of you receiving your parcel for the past one year.

> Meanwhile we are happy to inform you that FedEx
> International Courier Service has finally compromise with
> National Insurance Corporation in London and subsequently
> approved your parcel among the 24 valuable parcels to
> be couriered after the release of the parcels from NICON
> Insurance Company. Your parcel contains a cheque worth
> 500,000GBP (Five Hundred Thousand Great Britian Pounds).
> Due to the long scrutiny, your private residential address
> was not found and could not be retrived from our database.
> You can now re-send your residential address back to FedEx
> International Courier Service where your parcel can be
> delivered to you without any further hesitations.

Again, these e-mails are crafted by identity thieves, not Rhodes Scholars. It's important to remember that these e-mails are not hand-crafted for you, but are being sent to as many e-mail addresses as the scammer can come up with. From the criminal's perspective, it's a numbers game.

The scammers are familiar with human nature and will try almost anything they think will get their "readers" to spill their personal information. Here's another one aimed at lonely single men. It has all of the bad spelling and grammar of the Nigerian notes, but appeals to the heart instead of financial greed. These are usually accompanied by a stock photograph of an attractive model.

> Hello man my new friend!
>
> I understand, that you do not know me and I do not know
> you, but probably in the future all can change. All good always
> occurs in the future and I ask a few patience from you to
> read my letter up to the end. In the beginning I want to be
> presented you and to tell a little about my life.

My name is Kseniya and to me it will be very pleasant, if you will name me so. Was born 29 years ago and all this time I live in Russia, in city of Kirov. Now I work as the seller in shop and I very much like my work as I every day communicate with many different people. My life goes in regular intervals and every day is similar on previous.

I like my friends and love my family. Certainly the most important i want to found love and my the husband to be the happiest woman in the world. For all my life I could not meet the man to which I could trust completely and with which I would like to connect my life, but very much I want.

They gave to me yours E-mail and have told, that you also are interested to find the woman for a life. I think, that now you can understand, how my letter has come to you, could learn a little about my life and about me, but I do not know your desires and I ask to think.

We can try to build serious relations or probably simply to be friends. If you do not have desire simply speak to me and I can understand. Nevertheless if I am interesting to you it would be very pleasant for me to learn also a little more about you and to receive your photos.

I understand in computers not much, but I hope, that you also can receive my photos in this letter. Certainly appearance not the most important in the person both his private world and soul are of great value, but nevertheless it is more pleasant to receive the letter from the person and to see, how he looks. All this, that I wanted to tell to you and now I shall wait only your answer. Excuse, if I something have offended you in my letter or something has told not correctly, but understand, that I try it for the first time and I worry a little. Even if serious relations are not interesting to you or I am not pleasant, simply let to me know only to my personal e-mail: ***@***.com

Again, the point of this scam is to involve the reader in a conversation that will quickly, and naturally, turn to requests for more personal information.

Here's another approach that is very popular today. If you've posted e-mail contact information on a job search website, you've probably received something very similar:

Dear XXXXX XXXXX:

We have analyzed your resume and see you as a potential candidate of our firm.

You may learn about firm business activity on our website. We'd like to offer you the Financial Manager job.

You may also hold a job in another firm as our vacancy won't take much of your time.

Requirements for the Financial manager position:

- Well-timed encashment of the checks drawn on your name
- Monthly report under performed operations
- Work efficiency

Financial manager position obligations:

- 1–4 hours of time per week
- Over 22 years old
- THE CITIZENSHIP OF THE USA is a must.

Financial manager position payment:

- The first probation month - $XXXX (it'll grow in future)
- Every transaction's commission is not less than 10% (out of cashed check sum or out of sum entered to your account).

Our company undertakes to cover transmission, check clearance and all other expenses at its own cost.

If you agree to work for our company, it is necessary for you to:

1. Reply to this e-mail.
2. Provide your full name, home address and phone.

FILL IN YOUR DATA CORRECTLY.

You are to take the following steps in order to get down to work:

1. Log on our company site by the link click here
2. Check the ? REGISTRATION FINANCIAL MANAGER ? tab
3. Pass registration
4. Fill in the contract and send it at a specified address

After we check your data, there will start your cooperation with our business. You can also view all information in regard to the operation of our company on our website on the Internet.

Respectfully yours,
Manager XXXXX XXXXX

The appeal here is to out-of-work jobseekers. Again, if it looks too good to be true, it probably is. Most of the recipients of this e-mail have no background in finance at all, and this makes them unlikely candidates for the Financial Manager position. This scam can be easy to miss as there are also a lot of legitimate businesses selling franchises that are also "mining" job search websites for e-mail addresses.

The scams of the future are likely to be more personal and harder to spot than the barrage of badly worded e-mails you see today. It is already difficult to tell a legitimate note from a criminal come-on, and it's probably going to get worse before it gets better. Researchers are working on a number of solutions using cryptography, digital signatures, and other authentication techniques that are difficult to spoof. Unfortunately, as with most such efforts involving the digital infrastructure, hackers will probably have a slight edge over the security experts. Your best chance of avoiding this kind of fraud is to stay informed, pay attention to security alerts, and, above all, be skeptical.

04.

HIGH-TECH EXPLOITS—
AND HOW TO PREVENT THEM

The vast majority of identity theft does not require the use of high-tech gadgetry. Even some of the most popular Internet scams are merely updated versions of age-old con games, supercharged by the web's global reach and relative anonymity. Dumpster diving, receipt snatching, tricking someone into revealing their password, even copying massive databases onto a hard drive—none of these require more technical know-how than that of an average high school student.

That is not to say that there's nothing new under the sun—there certainly is. The communication capabilities of the Internet, which enable most of the scams we've looked at so far, are only one limited aspect of the overall technological revolution that has changed our society so dramatically over the past few decades. Banks, big businesses, media, and retailers have all seen their businesses change dramatically and conclusively over the past few years.

Identity theft is no exception. Most of us have not yet been touched by the effects of some of the newest developments in the field, but the day is surely coming when we will be. One of the seemingly immutable laws of scientific progress is that criminals are the first to develop clever ways to use new technologies while society spends most of its energy trying to catch up with the criminals.

Our contemporary commercial culture, with its rapid pace, instant communications, powerful computers, and sophisticated software, has proven to be fertile ground for the next generation of criminal behavior. Let's take a look at some of the most recent developments in this area, so that you know what to worry about next.

VIRUSES AND MALWARE

One way that hackers try to steal your information is to trick you into downloading a piece of corrupt software (known as a "trojan" or "malware") that installs a program, hidden deep in your computer's operating system, that searches your files for valuable information (like passwords or account information). Once the software has finished checking your files, it will "phone home" and send an electronic message containing the goods back to the hackers. One type of malicious software even has the ability to make copies of itself and mail them to the addresses in your address book or contact database, thereby sharing your problem with a constantly growing group of your friends and colleagues. After reading about phishing in the previous chapter, you probably know better than to click on an untrustworthy link in an e-mail. There is another good reason not to do this: Your click can open a web page that contains malicious program code. Just opening the page will install a small, carefully crafted program on your computer that allows the programmer to control it remotely.

Viruses and malware, though, are not restricted to hyperlinks in e-mails and have been found in almost every kind of file. They can be buried in a Microsoft Word document, a picture, or even MP3s. The thief's goal is to make the download look as attractive and innocent as possible.

Unfortunately, some companies have tried to use this kind of criminal action to protect their digital property rights in questionable ways. In 2005, Sony BMG added a piece of software to 50 of its music CDs. Each disk contained a hidden program known to hackers as a "rootkit." This rootkit was designed to hide itself deep within the operating system, covering up all traces of its installation. Once safely embedded, the program was designed to scan the target computer and send Sony a list of music found on the machine. Unfortunately, the code was poorly designed and ended up exposing the infected computers to attacks from others.

ZOMBIES, BOTS, AND BOTNETS

Once a hacker has gained control of your computer, it is referred to as a "zombie." A zombie computer appears to be normal, but the programmer has installed a code that allows her to control it remotely in the future. In most cases, your zombie will be triggered in combination with many other computers. At this point your computer is referred to as a "bot" and becomes part of a "botnet" when joined with other computers. A botnet is a group of compromised computers that can be launched en masse at a higher profile target, usually a computer belonging to a company or a government agency. These institutions typically have better security and encryption to protect against attacks. However, they can be broken into either by "cracking" the encryption using "brute force" (trying every reasonable option) or by a massed attack that overwhelms their defenses. As you can probably imagine, a password that would be impossible for a single person to figure out might yield to the combined computing power of thousands of zombie computers. Just like the proverbial roomful of monkeys, the zombies, acting in concert and centrally directed by the hacker, can mount a sophisticated attack that will break through most systems.

A cruder use of botnets is to execute a Denial of Service (DoS) attack against a high-profile target, to overwhelm the system's defenses, to cherry-pick valuable information, or to make a political statement. A DoS attack works by directing thousands of controlled computers to try to log into a host computer—or send certain low-level Internet messages—at the same time. This can tie up the target, or even drive the website out of commission for the duration of the attack. The consequences can be annoying or life-threatening depending on what kind of computer system is attacked.

This may not be identity theft in the traditional sense, but this kind of attack steals your computer's identity and uses it to commit crimes. At the very least, this remote control of your computer poses an extreme threat to the security of your personal information.

WI-FI HACKERS

Wireless networking is a wonderful thing. We use it at the workplace to untether our machines from our desks. We use it at home to extend our Internet reach throughout the house without resorting to expensive wiring. We even use it when we're out in public or traveling. Laptops would be far less useful without Wi-Fi. Newer gadgets like iPhones and Blackberries work faster and cheaper over wireless networks than they do on cellular networks. Many storefronts, restaurants, and coffeehouses offer free Wi-Fi for customers.

The downside to this newly networked environment is that it offers yet another avenue for criminals to access your computers. Home and small business networks are routinely targeted by "demon drivers," people who travel around neighborhoods looking for unprotected networks to tap into. If they can join your network, they may be able to access your computer hard drive, and any information on it.

Any portable wireless device can be invaded if not sufficiently protected. Some popular levels of password protection, for example, can be defeated by persistent criminals armed with a computer capable of testing thousands of different passwords against the system. Although technically difficult, wireless hacking has the huge advantage (for the criminal!) of being nearly untraceable. The notorious TJX incident—discussed in the next chapter—occurred because the identity thieves intercepted a weakly encrypted wireless signal from several of the company's stores and copied credit card information for millions of consumers.

PACKET SNIFFING

The growth of the Internet into a multimedia information utility has been one of the most dramatic changes in our culture over the past decade or two. At some level, though, Internet traffic is just a string of numbers that get routed through many computers and locations (hence the name *router*) on its way to its destination. You would probably be surprised to find out how many stops your communications have to make along the way—most traffic makes it through at least seven to ten "hops." At any one of these "hops," or transfer points, criminals can attach hardware or software that "sniffs," or listens, to the information and then analyzes and stores a copy of whatever you transmit.

The government does this routinely under the auspices of various post-9/11 counter-intelligence programs, but private individuals can too if they have access to one of the Internet's routing points or a machine on your home or corporate network. These sniffer programs are legal to own and freely available on the Internet, and it's for this reason that you need to be sure your communications are secure before you type any critical information (like a credit card number) into your browser. This requires setting up a secure communications session, something that online banking systems usually do automatically. Different browsers indicate a secure session in different ways, although most display a lock icon to indicate that your communications are safe.

SKIMMERS

Skimmers are thieves who steal credit card numbers, either manually from a receipt or by using a special electronic device to copy or "skim" the number. The electronic version of skimming usually involves a handheld device that a renegade store clerk or waiter can use to surreptitiously scan credit cards. The device often includes a small keypad so the card's security code can also be captured. Other skimming devices can be attached to the card-swiping slot at a cash register or ATM, although the criminal will still need to intercept the user's PIN. Skimming makes it possible to harvest account numbers and IDs from hundreds, if not thousands, of customers at a time. Stop & Shop supermarkets, for example, discovered that more than 1000 of its customers lost their debit card information to criminals who replaced the stores' card-swiping equipment with skimming devices. The thieves were able to make off with more than $100,000 in fraudulent ATM withdrawals before the scheme was detected.

CELL PHONE "CLONING"

One specialized application of skimming takes advantage of the cell phone networks' ability to remotely check the identity of a cell phone. It only takes two numbers to identify a phone: the Electronic Serial Number and the Mobile Identification Number. If thieves can get their hands on these two numbers, they can implant, or "burn," them into a second phone. The second phone will look identical to the cell phone network, but the bills will still go to the owner of the original phone. Fortunately, it's not that easy to get the ID numbers by physically checking the phone. Thieves try to get them by hacking into the cell network system, or by eavesdropping ("sniffing") on the network. These techniques work better on older phones, but they have not yet been shown to work against GSM phones like the Apple's iPhone or RIM's Blackberry models.

RFID CHIPS

A new technology called RFID chips, designed to be a replacement for bar codes, also has the potential to become a new and troublesome tool for snooping on personal information. These chips, which can be as small as a grain of rice, are embedded into all kinds of packaging to identity the item for inventory, shipping, and point-of-sale devices. Researchers are still working out new ways and places to use RFID technology, and the U.S. government is requiring all new U.S. passports to have these chips embedded in their covers.

The good news is that this should speed up a number of inconvenient and time-consuming practices, and the coordination between government databases and airport security is only one example.

From a cyber-thieves' point of view, the big advantage of these chips is that it's much easier to read an RFID chip from thirty feet away than a bar code. A skimmer doesn't even have to get close to the passport to read its information. RFID proponents are looking to expand the technology's use throughout the commercial infrastructure, in which case their "skim-ability" could turn out to be a huge problem.

After reading this, you may be worried about using the Internet, but identity theft encompasses more than just the online world. The best way to arm yourself is with knowledge, so read on through the next few chapters of the book, which offer a look at how you can combat these threats to your security.

05.

INSTITUTIONAL EXPOSURE—AND HOW TO STEER CLEAR OF IT

You may be thinking, "I was careful. I shredded every credit card receipt, practiced good computer security, and didn't give my personal information to anyone, but I still got robbed! How can that be?"

That's because there's at least one more major problem area that is completely outside of your control—institutional data breaches.

One of the most troubling developments in the modern era of online commerce is the incredible growth of massive corporate or institutional databases that contain unprecedented amounts of sensitive personal information.

CORPORATE DATA BREACHES

Corporations store enormous amounts of our personal information. Some of it comes from online shopping, but most of it is the electronic byproduct of administrative procedures such as building marketing databases, analyzing customer transactions, and storing financial account information. These sensitive computer systems are routinely exposed, either deliberately by hackers or accidentally by employees. Regardless of the motivation, these breaches always affect a great number of people, often many millions.

In 2007, for example, retail giant TJX (parent company of Marshalls, TJ Maxx, and Winners) was hit by a security breach that exposed at least 46 million customers' financial and personal information. In this case, unsecured transaction information from retail stores loaded with customers' personal data was intercepted by hackers. Like most breaches, corporate negligence was at least partly responsible.

Many affected customers didn't even have accounts with the stores! Their only mistake was buying something at a TJX store with a credit card. As compensation to their customers, TJX had a customer appreciation day in January 2009, offering storewide sales of 15 percent off.

In 2008, a potentially bigger data breach story took place involving Heartland Payment systems, a credit and debit card transaction processor. The company was hacked, possibly exposing the financial information of customers of over 160 banks.

The Privacy Rights Clearinghouse has documented over 900 individual data breaches by U.S. companies and government agencies since January 2005. Together these breaches have involved over 200 million total records containing sensitive personal information—many containing Social Security numbers.

COMPANIES THAT SELL YOUR DATA

Not only is your data stored in these massive databases, but it's often for sale as well.

Data marketing is extremely profitable, since so many businesses are willing to pay for your information: to decide whether to extend credit, to write an insurance policy, to offer employment, or even to check on you before you're allowed on an airplane.

A number of companies, including many that you probably haven't heard of, make their money by compiling your personal information into "dossiers" they can sell to other marketers. This includes information on what you buy, where you live, what causes you contribute to, or even what magazines you subscribe to. All of this information is added up, blended together, and put up for sale, and there's not a thing you can do about it.

The credit bureaus, which I'll look at more closely in Part II of this book, are somewhat regulated. There are, however, many services that can deliver the goods on your identity—for a fee—without being hampered by any regulations at all.

The low-end services are available to almost anyone. You can find plenty of advertisements for them online at sites that let you search for addresses or phone numbers. For a $50–$100 fee they will put together a background report on you based on publicly available sources. Although they don't include financial account information, they can usually provide your name, address, education, and employment. Some even display driver's license information, Social Security numbers, listings of real estate transactions, court actions—whatever's available from public records.

The higher-powered services are usually subscription-based and make some effort to validate that the person doing the checking has a legitimate reason to do so. Unfortunately, a large number of people and businesses use these systems and there are limits to how carefully they all can be checked. This, in turn, opens the door to identity thieves.

One good example is Acxiom (*www.acxiom.com*), based in Conway, Arkansas. They maintain records on almost every American, but they collect far more than just account information. They are a data warehouse for the retail industry and store information on your reading habits, health problems, buying patterns, food preferences, and other personal data that marketers want to know. They claim to conduct 125,000 background checks monthly and store worldwide demographic information on 500 million individuals. And they have had problems with their computers. Acxiom was hacked in 2003, exposing as many as 1.6 billion data records containing names, addresses, e-mail addresses, and other consumer information.

Another example is Choicepoint, a spinoff from credit bureau Experian, that is often used as a private intelligence agency by both the private sector and the government. Choicepoint has seen revenue of upwards of a billion dollars and has information on over 250 million Americans. They buy data, including credit reports and driver's records, from a multitude of sources and collect it into a substantial electronic dossier. For a fee, they will conduct computerized background checks that reveal far more information than what appears on a credit report. Like the rest of the companies in this category, Choicepoint is unregulated.

In 2005, Choicepoint had a well-publicized incident where identity thieves set up several fake businesses and opened up accounts with the company. These phony companies then used that access to retrieve data on over 150,000 people who were subsequently targeted for identity theft. The whole matter only became public when the company was forced to notify the 35,000 affected Californians thanks to a state law requiring the mandatory disclosure of data breaches affecting consumers.

Choicepoint also offers a service called AutoTrackXP, which many law enforcement officers use to locate suspects. The AutoTrackXP website describes the service as follows: "Using as little information as a name, AutoTrackXP cross-references an enormous amount of data—addresses, driver's licenses, property deed transfers, corporate information and much more—and unifies it into a single, easy-to-read report. It can even access real-time phone listings and perform on-demand court record searches."

The main problem with this kind of service is that its sheer size makes it difficult to regulate. Given the number of records and the number of people who have access to them, it's almost inevitable that some kind of breach will occur. There is also the very real concern that a hacker or a disgruntled employee of this kind of database company might steal records en masse and sell them to professional identity thieves.

DATA SWAPPING

One of the most troubling aspects of the hyper-growth of databases is the shameless swapping of data that happens behind the closed doors of consumer-oriented companies. Many retail companies have turned to partnerships and alliances with other companies as a way to build their business. If you read the privacy policies of the companies you do business with you'll notice that most of them reserve the right to share your information with "partners" or "affiliates." What this really means is that they may enter into marketing agreements with other companies who are allowed to copy and merge their databases. Your identity is then vulnerable to the new organizations that have access to these expanded databases. Obviously, this increases the vulnerability of the original database—more people, more access, different security systems, and little or no regulation.

BIG GOVERNMENT

The government is the biggest collector of personal information. Every federal agency and state and municipal government keeps lists of their citizens indexed by Social Security number. The SSN is, as we've discussed, your biggest point of exposure to identity theft. There have been innumerable incidents involving government data breaches of private information, most involving inadvertent disclosures of lists of citizens sorted by SSN.

This type of pattern extends to all kinds of government collection information. It's a little-known fact, for example, that many states sell access to their Department of Motor Vehicles records in bulk. This includes not only driving records, but also personal information like addresses, telephone numbers, and sometimes photographs.

The more personal information the government collects and stores in its computer systems and the more integrated that those databases become, the likelier it is that there will be breaches of privacy. Although there are policy safeguards, they are mostly ineffective because the penalties are minor and are aimed primarily at the person responsible for the mistake—not at the managers who direct security and privacy policies.

The federal government's database initiatives, combined with the consolidation of law enforcement databases since September 11, 2001, have made it much easier for millions of government employees and their affiliated contractors to see, lose, or even steal your personal information.

In 2006, a single laptop carried home by a civil servant working for the Department of Veterans Affairs was stolen, exposing over 26 million

Americans, all of them military veterans, to the threat of identity theft. The computer contained names, birthdays, and Social Security numbers and, as we've seen, that is more than enough information for thieves to do damage with.

The punishment for this careless government employee? Administrative leave. Although the laptop was recovered later that year, it is impossible to know whether or not the data was copied. In 2009, the government announced a $20 million class action lawsuit had been filed by the affected veterans and offered to pay between $75 and $1,500 to each person who could demonstrate that they'd been harmed by the theft.

The VA case underscores one of the main reasons why identity theft is so easy today: Digital data is easy to store, transport, and manipulate. The cost to copy even large amounts of data is trivial; you can purchase a one terabyte hard drive, capable of easily holding the key information for every single American citizen today, for less than $100.

Unfortunately, the world we live in today is flooded with personal information. Your efforts to protect your data may often seem futile, like trying to stop a rising river with leaking sandbags, but this doesn't mean you're helpless. Fraud made possible by identity theft may come from every direction, but with few exceptions they always move toward the same target—your financial assets. So even though you can't control inadvertent data breaches or protect data-mining corporations from their own security flaws, you can protect yourself by carefully monitoring your credit history and other financial information. Part II of this book will focus on how best to protect your interests. In the next chapter, though, we'll take a quick look at why identity thieves want your identity, and what they're going to do with it.

06.

WHAT THEY'RE DOING WITH YOUR IDENTITY

Although all thieves are after money, they use your identity to get it in different ways, ranging from the simple and direct to the devious and complex. One of the worst things about having your identity stolen is the fear that the thief may be taking advantage of your identity in ways you're not aware of. The fear that you could wake up one day facing civil or criminal legal action for something you didn't do is just as powerful as the fear that you could wake up one day penniless because your accounts have been looted.

I can't tell you that your fears are completely unfounded because it's difficult to predict just what criminals will do with your information. But the vast majority of cases turn out to involve financial frauds. They want to take advantage of your identity to make as much money as they can off of it. With that in mind, let's take a look at some of the most common ways identity thieves misuse other people's identities.

CREDIT CARD FRAUD

In 2003, singer Ruben Studdard won a $2 million lawsuit against Ronald W. Edwards, his former manager, and Edwards' promotions company, Sez Inc., for identity theft. According to the court ruling, Edwards had applied for credit cards in Studdard's name and then bought goods totaling over $100,000. He also wrote $150,000 worth of checks to himself from Studdard's accounts and deposited another $22,000 of stolen checks into his own account. Edwards was able to do this because he apparently forged power of attorney documents using Studdard's signature. Even in today's electronic age, a physical signature is often all that's needed to steal an identity.

It's easier for a thief to get money using your credit card than from your bank account because, for one thing, he doesn't need your PIN. The thief also knows that you're not going to be liable for the credit charges (only up to $50 per card) if you report it promptly. The assumption is that you won't pursue the theft as vigorously if you're not on the hook for the money.

Credit card fraud takes two forms: taking over an existing account or requesting new cards in your name. The first is simple, based on the theft of your wallet or pocketbook. The second is more difficult and troubling because the thief needs either access to your mailbox to intercept the new cards or the ability to change your address of record so the cards can be sent elsewhere. As a result, a thief trying to get new cards may be someone you know.

BANK ACCOUNT THEFT

This can happen in a number of ways. A thief may have stolen some of your bank checks or she might have stolen your ATM card and "cloned" it (copied the electronic information from the magnetic strip onto a blank card). Your bank account can also be looted if a thief gains access to it online and withdraws the money via Electronic Funds Transfer (ETF). Online banking systems are usually protected by account numbers and passwords—which are susceptible to some of the simple techniques we looked at earlier—dumpster diving, stealing password lists, etc.

TELEPHONE, CABLE, AND OTHER KINDS OF UTILITY FRAUD

Thieves who try to use your accounts to pay their utility bills are easier to catch because the service has to be delivered to a physical address, providing a pretty good clue to the thieves' identity. This is one of the cases the police might investigate because there's a chance that it could lead to an arrest. Portable services such as cell phones are a little more problematic, however, because they don't have a fixed physical address.

EMPLOYMENT FRAUD

There have been cases in which people have stolen identities in order to get a job. If you start getting strange e-mails or see an unfamiliar employment entry on your credit report, it's possible someone is using your name to hold down a job. To accomplish this, the thief would need to discover a little bit of your background info and your Social Security number. Keep in mind that there is a big market in the United States for stolen Social Security numbers, since immigrants can use them to get work permits.

As discussed earlier, job search sites can also trigger requests for personal information purportedly for employment purposes.

SOCIAL SECURITY AND PENSION FRAUD

Lucyna Turyk-Wawrynowicz became infamous in 2006 for stealing from her celebrity clients, among them Robert DeNiro and Candice Bergen, but she got her job to begin with by stealing the Social Security number of a little girl to get the necessary papers to work in the United States. Along with a $96,000 pair of diamond earrings belonging to DeNiro's wife Grace Hightower and a $1,000 leather jacket belonging to Bergen, she also stole credit cards and used them to go on several shopping sprees at Barneys, a famous New York clothing store.

An identity thief can try to use your Social Security number to apply for government-paid benefits that you have not applied for yet. This kind of fraud is more common than you think, even given that cashing or depositing government checks leaves a pretty clear trail to the thief. In most cases, this particular kind of fraud is perpetrated by someone you know—a friend, relative, or neighbor who has access to your mailbox. Because it involves the mail, it is a federal crime and will be investigated.

In a well-publicized action in 2006, over 1,000 U.S. Citizenship and Immigration officers arrested hundreds of illegal workers in the meat-packing business in six states. The workers had used stolen Social Security numbers to get fake work certificates.

Ricky Gervais, star of the BBC's *The Office* and HBO's *Extras*, had his identity stolen in 2007 by thieves who siphoned money from his bank account to buy gold. The bizarre part of the theft was the fake ID that the con men created. They cut out his picture from a DVD box of the British version of *The Office* and stuck it on a dead man's passport. The thieves used a stolen bank password to transfer nearly $380,000 from Gervais's account to a bullion dealer as payment for 60 pounds of gold bars. They planned to use the passport as identification when they picked up the precious metal. Fortunately for the comedian, the bullion dealer was suspicious and called the police. Officers were waiting for the crooks when they showed up to claim the gold.

GOVERNMENT DOCUMENT FRAUD

With your Social Security number and a little background info, thieves can apply for official documents in your name such as birth certificates, driver's licenses, and even passports. It can be a difficult crime to spot because there's rarely anything to alert you to their use of the documents. If you do receive mail confirming your application for such sensitive personal documents, alert the issuing authority immediately. Identity thieves need these documents to either hide from prosecution or, more commonly, to provide documentation for illegal aliens.

MEDICAL SERVICES FRAUD

It can be easy to steal medical services if someone gets a hold of your health insurance identification number. Doctors' offices rarely require any identification for new patients beyond the policy number and, if the thief keeps up with the co-pay charges, he is unlikely to be caught. Unless, of course, you notice delivery of service confirmations for treatments or procedures that you didn't receive, or the health plan administrators notice that you are receiving similar services from two different doctors. Although this type of theft doesn't come directly out of your pocket, it does contribute to the skyrocketing cost of medical care. It is also common for policyholders to share Medicare or Medicaid credentials, and this also contributes to costs.

STOLEN IDENTITIES AND LAW ENFORCEMENT

What do Renee A. White of Ohio, Jeff Goldsmith of Indiana, Christie Scalzo of Nevada, and Hilario Mercado of Illinois have in common? Each of them was arrested because the thief who had stolen their identity committed a crime and gave their stolen ID to the arresting officers. In each case, a warrant was issued for their arrest. Each of them had trouble convincing the authorities of his or her innocence. Like other identity theft victims caught in similar circumstances, they had to go through the arrest booking and, in a few cases, incarceration before they could argue their case before a judge.

A thief can show stolen ID when she's booked and have a pretty good chance of getting away with a crime because most police forces do not cross-check identity paperwork. This can be one of the most painful forms of victimization because most people don't know that anything has happened until they've been arrested. A simple traffic stop can turn into a night in jail if the arresting officer discovers an outstanding warrant when he calls in your ID. As you can imagine, the argument that, "It wasn't me, officer!" doesn't go over especially well with the police, and it can be very difficult to prove that your identity has been stolen.

ONLINE FRAUD

We covered some of the most common forms of this in the last few chapters, and it's clear that we all have too many online accounts. As a result, most people need to keep a written list of accounts and passwords that is easy to lose or have stolen. The other problem with online accounts is that few of us check the transactions as carefully as we check our printed bills, giving identity thieves a better chance of getting away with fraud. It's also important to remember that identity thieves are good at guessing passwords from the information they have available. (More on choosing good passwords later in the book.)

Even worse, many people use the same password for all of their online accounts. If a thief discovers one of your passwords, he or she can try it at other heavily used sites to see if you've reused the same password somewhere else.

The uses for a stolen identity are almost endless, and clever identity thieves develop new ones every day. This section of the book makes it clear just how many different kinds of fraud you have to be alert for once your identity has been stolen. I hope it also explains why I'm so insistent about the need to protect your identity and to take aggressive action to "rehabilitate" it once it has been stolen.

PART II

WHAT TO DO WHEN YOUR IDENTITY IS STOLEN

07.

HOW TO TELL IF YOUR IDENTITY HAS BEEN STOLEN

Tim Goodwin hadn't received his MasterCard statement for three months. Finally he called his credit card company. The company representative told him that they had been mailing the statements to the correct address. Tim wondered if maybe someone else in the apartment building had been getting his mail by accident. Acting on the advice of a lawyer friend, he pulled his credit report from Experian and went over it carefully.

He immediately noticed a flurry of charges made in the last few weeks that he was sure weren't his. They were all coming from Seattle, which was odd because Tim lived in San Mateo. The items purchased were also all wrong. He'd never bought parts for a Harley in his life. Heck, he'd never even owned a motorcycle! And he certainly had never spent $300 in a tattoo parlor!

EARLY WARNINGS

How can you tell if your identity has been stolen? And, hopefully, in time to prevent a serious loss?

Many times, of course, victims of identity theft—like Sarah Gonzalez and her Macy's account, or Tim Goodwin and his MasterCard—find out the hard way: when an identity thief has successfully inflicted serious damage to both their finances and their credit history.

One of the major problems of dealing with identity theft is that the thieves, in most cases, steal intangible assets—such as copies of your account numbers and passwords—rather than tangible objects like cash or cars or silverware. Sometimes it's impossible to know whether you're really a victim until incontrovertible events—like a large negative number on an account balance or a string of charges for motorcycle parts—give the crime away.

What should you do if you think your personal information is at risk but you don't know if it's really been stolen?

Maybe you've lost your wallet, been notified that a company you do business with has inadvertently exposed personal data on a website, or lost a laptop holding customer data. Maybe you've even gotten a phone call asking you to confirm some personal details or visited a website that required more information than usual and turned out not to be what it pretended to be.

These can all be "early warnings" of identity theft, but you really can't be sure if your information has fallen into the wrong hands, or if it's being used to try to impersonate you.

Because you don't know if a crime has been committed, there are limits to what you can do. There are a few important steps that you should take just in case the problem turns out to be more serious.

First of all, make sure you follow up on the problems that you do know about. If your wallet never turns up or a phone or laptop that contains personal information goes missing, you should assume it's been stolen. Report the theft to the police, to your bank (if you've lost a debit card or account information), and to the fraud departments of the issuers of any credit card that's missing. Most companies are very responsive to this kind of report, and will give you new cards and account numbers quickly.

The next step is to be more vigilant and organized about your finances, your accounts, and your identity. In most cases, the steps you must take are very similar to what you'd do if your identity had actually been stolen—these are covered in more detail in the following chapter.

Pull your credit reports from all three of the major agencies and examine them for inconsistencies. Look for and report anything unusual: address changes, name changes, accounts you don't recognize, or new charges on inactive accounts.

You are entitled to one free report from each agency every year. One strategy is to stagger the three free reports, getting one from a different bureau every four months. This way you can track your credit for a full year at no cost. If you've received notice of a data breach, the offending business will usually offer you a free report. Make sure you take advantage of it.

Pay closer attention to your monthly account statements than you usually do. Look for unusual charges or transactions, and ask the credit company for more details on any you can't identify. Make a list of your accounts, and make sure that you're receiving statements from all of them on a regular basis.

Start a file and document everything. Your goal is to keep a careful watch on your accounts so that you can spot real trouble as early as possible. Make sure to read Part III of this book to find the best ways to prevent identity theft from happening to you in the future.

Unfortunately, this kind of monitoring is pretty much all you can do unless and until you find evidence that a real crime has occurred. Don't panic, and don't do anything drastic like changing your Social Security number. Trying to create a totally new "financial identity" for yourself can create its own significant problems.

TELL-TALE SIGNS OF IDENTITY THEFT

If your personal information really has been compromised and is being used for criminal purposes, you're likely to see one or more of the following signs of identity theft. Any of these should be followed up on and resolved in an active and aggressive way. (Again, the following chapter offers a more complete guide on how to respond.) Remember, these could be the only signs you'll get of imminent identity crimes, and you'll need to act as soon as you can to limit the damage.

You Get Mail You Didn't Expect or Can't Explain

If criminals have taken over your identity, they're doing it for a reason—usually a financial one. They are secretly plotting how to turn your good name into cash or tangible goods. In the process of doing so, they may inadvertently cause an unexpected or inexplicable notice, invoice, or receipt to be sent to your home. If you receive anything suspicious in your mail, be sure to follow up on it. Call or contact the organization listed on the document to find out why it was sent. Maybe it really is a mistake. Or maybe it's just the tip of the iceberg, and you are on the *Titanic*.

The same applies to telephone calls. Unfortunately, the first unusual phone calls you'll receive will be from collection agencies. In most cases an identity thief will have bought something using your good credit and failed to pay the bill, thus triggering an unwarranted debt collection action. Collection actions you didn't incur are one of the most painful aspects of identity theft because they can ruin your credit as you try to establish your innocence.

You Don't Get Mail You Did Expect

Sometimes thieves who have stolen existing account information change the mailing address so they receive the bills and other correspondence from the finance company. This makes it easier for them to change the PIN or the password that "unlocks" the account. Credit companies and banks insist on mailing new account info and new credit or debit cards to your address of record. Once the thieves have changed that address, they will be able to receive and confirm new credit cards or changes to the account—in other words, almost everything they need to steal your money.

The natural tendency is to enjoy any respite from our bills. Unfortunately, waiting for a few months to see whether a bill eventually shows up can also delay your discovery of a misappropriated account. Be on the lookout for regular bills that don't arrive. If you don't get a bill you are expecting, call the company and ask if it has been sent out. If the answer is yes, you may be the victim of identity theft.

All of your mail may be redirected in some cases, and this is a simple matter of filing a change-of-address card with the Post Office. While most people will notice a lack of any mail at all almost immediately, it also means that a potential identity thief may gain access to all of your accounts, and wreak widespread havoc.

You Find Strange Entries on Your Credit Report

The only surefire way to determine if you have been the victim of identity theft is by constantly monitoring your credit reports. Although this will not protect you from having your identity stolen, it may let you know if it's already happened.

The first few times you pull your reports and scan them are good opportunities to fix incorrect information. Challenge everything that's wrong on the report, including bad addresses, incorrect information about accounts, and closed or forgotten accounts. Once you've done this a few times and the corrected information has worked its way through the credit bureaucracy, you will have established a clean and reliable information baseline for yourself.

Now you can just look for new information. If a new entry appears and you have no idea what it is, investigate the transaction. Be aware that in many cases the reporting entity on a credit report may be different from the one to whom you actually incurred the debt. For example, mortgage lenders routinely "sell" your home loan to someone else. Even if you don't recognize the name, you should recognize the amount and type of transaction. If something completely new turns up, it's time to get worried.

If you find something on your report that you don't understand, contact the company listed on the report and see if they can shed some light on the charge. If you aren't responsible for the transaction or still don't understand it, you are probably the victim of identity theft. You should immediately treat it as such and follow the steps listed in the next chapter. Bear in mind that there's a considerable lag time involved in the credit reporting process. When it first shows up on a report, the actual theft is at least thirty days old. A lot of other damage may already have been done—damage that just hasn't been reported yet. The sooner you get started, the sooner you can start preventing a big problem from turning into an insurmountable one.

You Find Strange Entries on an Account Statement

An identity thief's first act, typically, is to try to exploit your existing accounts. If he's gotten any of your credit card numbers, it's not too hard to use them to charge purchases against your account.

You have some protection if this occurs. Credit companies generally limit your losses from credit card fraud to $50 if you notify them promptly that it's been lost or stolen. Also, many vendors will only ship a charged product to the billing address of record. Knowing this, identity thieves tend to buy things that don't have to be shipped and aren't too expensive.

When you check your statement, look for unusual purchases that seem to fall into this pattern. Don't let even a small amount go unchallenged. Often professional identity thieves test out an account by making a small purchase. This "carding" often takes the form of making a small online purchase to see if a stolen credit card is still valid. If successful, they will follow with larger purchases.

You See Strange Transactions on an Online Account or Get Odd (Non-Spam) E-mail

Most people today are buying more and more things on the Internet. Some of us have online accounts that we use regularly, like Amazon.com or iTunes. For experienced identity thieves, these accounts are relatively easy to "break into" because they only require a user ID and a password. In many cases, the goods are digital, not physical, and can be immediately downloaded, circumventing the address-of-record protection you enjoy when buying physical goods.

The good news is that you'll usually notice this kind of thing faster, often within days of the theft, because most online vendors send you e-mail confirmation of the charges. If you get a confirmation for a charge you didn't make, immediately contact the fraud department of the online company and tell them what happened. They will usually rescind the charge and help you take action to protect your account.

Sometimes you'll get e-mails—purportedly from an online vendor such as eBay or PayPal—alerting you to an identity theft or a problem with your account. Unfortunately, these are almost always fakes, or phishing attacks, trying to convince you to turn over your account information to fix the situation. In fact, your information will go straight into the hands of the identity thieves. Such e-mails usually concern banking or financial information rather than products such as iTunes, since thieves are in it for cold, hard cash and not MP3 files.

Although authentic vendors do occasionally contact their customers via e-mail, sometimes even alerting them to possible security problems, they will almost never try to get you to "authenticate" yourself by entering your information. If you have any doubt whatsoever, contact the company by other means or contact them through their website rather than using the links in the e-mail.

You're Inexplicably Denied Credit

One of the most common ways you may find out that your identity has been stolen, unfortunately, is the hard way—you're denied new credit. This happens because a thief has stolen your identity, opened credit accounts, not paid the bills, and the creditor has dinged your credit report.

If you are denied credit because of a bad credit report, legally the creditor must tell you that this is the reason and that you are entitled to a free credit report. Get a copy of your report (which can be done online), contact any businesses that have contributed negative information to the report, and figure out if the denial is a simple mistake or the consequence of theft. If you are a victim of identity theft, turn directly to the next chapter for the steps you need to follow to get your identity back.

You Bounce a Check or a Credit Card Transaction Is Turned Down Unexpectedly

This is the way most people find out that they have a problem. You may discover there is less money in a bank account than you think there should be, or maybe your credit card is declined when you're buying something even though you know you're up to date with your payments. If this occurs while you're in a public place—a store or a restaurant, for example—it can be highly embarrassing and upsetting, not to mention inconvenient if you're the one trying to pay for dinner!

Do contact your financial institution as soon as possible to see what the problem is. Don't assume that it's just sloppy bookkeeping on your part—it could be a clear indication of a much more serious problem. There are legitimate reasons for a "good" credit card to be declined. For example, some cards aren't usable in a foreign country, and some banks will put a hold on your account if they see activity from an unusual place—such as a different state or country.

Identity thieves who steal from bank or credit card accounts tend to make as many charges as they can as quickly as they can. They know it won't take long for you to discover the problem and deactivate the card or the account. You need to move just as quickly to try to control the damage.

FIGHT BACK!

If you've experienced any of the "symptoms" described above, chances are you are a victim of identity theft. Unfortunately, the more sophisticated—and complicated—our financial institutions and their computer systems become, the more likely this is to happen to you. Fortunately, there are also an increasing number of ways to combat this kind of theft. If you are a victim of identity theft, turn directly to the next chapter for the steps you need to follow to get your identity back.

08.

HOW DO YOU GET YOUR IDENTITY BACK?

You have just found out that your identity has been stolen. Maybe you discovered it on your credit report; maybe you got a phone call from someone telling you that you haven't paid a bill you didn't know you had. Maybe you experienced one of the other scenarios outlined in the last chapter. In any case, you're sure that somewhere out there someone is using your personal information to steal money. What do you do now?

The most significant problem is that, although there are things you can and should do immediately to protect yourself, it may take months or years to fully restore your reputation. And it is unlikely that you will ever have the satisfaction of finding out who stole your identity.

The fact that identity theft has become so common is also a problem. If you expect your local law enforcement to treat the incident like a *CSI* case, you might as well forget it. Detectives will not come to your door to take your statement. You'll have to find out which office, or which officer, covers identity crimes for your local police department and make an appointment to see them. Your interaction with the police will probably be limited to filing a report on the crime and getting a case number from them to use with your insurance company or the credit agencies. When you call the credit bureaus to file your report, you probably won't be talking to a person; you'll be button pushing your way through an automated menu system.

Even worse, when you try to explain to your creditors that it's not your fault that you still owe them money because your identity was stolen, you're probably not going to get a lot of sympathy. Financial institutions and other business are losing so much money to identity thieves that they are not going to let you off the hook easily. Working your way through resolving the damage caused by an identity theft can be a lonely road to travel. Your friends will be sympathetic, but most of the people and institutions you deal with are going to be apathetic at best.

You need to understand from the outset that no one can fix this problem but you. It's your identity, and if you don't take care of it, no one else can or will. Starting immediately, you have to take on a new job; one that you might end up holding on to for a long time: fixing your own identity problems.

THE FOUR KEYS TO SURVIVING IDENTITY THEFT

This new job comes with four major responsibilities:

1. Getting organized, and keeping careful records.
2. Working with law enforcement to document the crime.
3. Working with credit bureaus to minimize the effect on your credit.
4. Work with individual creditors to repair your relationships.

Like most new jobs, your new responsibilities will require you to learn some new skills. You will be working with new people and unfamiliar institutions. It will require patience, diplomacy, and persistence. You'll be dealing with parts of the commercial and financial world that don't necessarily believe the customer is always right. In fact, their attitude may strike you as quite the opposite. The skills you learn, and the experience you gain, will prove to be invaluable both in repairing the damage caused by identity theft, and in being an informed and savvy participant in our high-tech, database-driven, big business and big government–run society.

We'll look at each of these areas in greater detail. It's important to remember, though, that you're still not done even after you've completed some of the actions I've described. You'll probably have to repeat some or all of them for a long time—a few years at least—before you resolve the problem completely. Cleaning up after an identity theft is not easy or quick. But it is absolutely necessary as your credit rating, and in many ways your future happiness depend on it.

TASK ONE:
GET ORGANIZED

The first thing you should do is to set up files to help you stay on task and on course with your identity recovery initiative. You can do a lot of this organizing electronically but, because you'll be collecting so many documents, it really helps to set up a physical filing system as well. So keep a hard file and put all correspondence related to the theft into this file. Careful record keeping is so important to your eventual success that you need to start thinking about it from the very beginning. You need to react quickly, efficiently, and effectively. You'll find yourself talking to different people at different organizations, all of whom will need slightly different information. You may end up sending slightly different stacks of copied documents to each of your contacts.

It's vitally important that you keep track of who needs what, where each form and document is, who has responded to you and what they've said, and, especially, who hasn't responded and what you need to do to get their attention.

Repairing your credit is almost always a long and drawn-out process. Incomplete record keeping can sometimes force you to start over on some aspects of it, and NOTHING is more difficult than trying to get a financial institution or a creditor to recreate a document that's gone missing in your files.

With good records, you can keep the process moving in the right direction—no matter how long or how complicated it becomes.

At a minimum your files should include:

- Copies of any credit reports you've received from the three different bureaus
- Copies of all correspondence initiated by you to credit bureaus, banks, credit card companies, or any other creditors
- Copies of all correspondence addressed to you by creditors, collection agencies, or reporting bureaus
- Copies of police reports
- A log of any telephone calls you've made while attempting to clear up the theft, including the date and time of the calls and the subjects discussed. Don't try to rely on your memory. You'll find it's nearly impossible to keep track of, among other things, new and old account numbers, changing company policies, or negotiations with individuals over the time it takes to resolve a case of identity theft.
- A list of organizations you've contacted along with the best contact information you've been able to get
- A time and expense log where you log your actions and track the money you've spent trying to resolve the issue. It's possible that you'll be able to recover some of your costs if your case ends up being solved.
- A working "to do" list that helps you stay on task and helps you follow up on outstanding correspondence or documentation

The specifics of how you organize this file aren't as important as putting something together that works for you and that you will actually use. You can keep the information in file folders, notebooks, binders, or in a neat pile on your desk; just don't avoid doing it or you run the risk of facing insurmountable problems down the road.

You're going to have to turn into a much more organized person than you've ever been before. Send all of your correspondence by certified mail and request a return receipt. Staple all of the return receipt stubs to copies of the correspondence and keep them in your files.

Never send originals to anyone if you can help it. If they misplace an original document (and sometimes they have good reasons to do so) it will be very difficult for you to pursue your claims. If you are required to deliver originals, get copies notarized and send them instead.

Your phone log should be as comprehensive as possible. Keep careful notes on every phone call you make about the theft, including the time and date of the call, the content of the conversation, and the name of the person(s) you talked to. If you speak with a police officer, ask for his or her badge number and the case number that's been assigned to the theft. The same is true for any organization: identifying the person to whom you're talking and, if you can, their direct extension or phone number so that you bypass their voice menu system in the future.

It's also important to keep detailed records of the expenses you incur and hours you spend on fixing the identity theft as well as any damages you suffer as a result of it. If the credit reporting agencies you deal with violate the Federal Credit Reporting Act (FCRA), there may come a time when you have grounds to go to court. If you do, you will need these records to convince the court to award damages.

Also, keep notes in your log detailing any non-monetary trouble that you experienced as a result of the identity theft. A court may factor in the emotional hassle caused by the theft when deciding whether to grant you a cash award.

Fill out a copy of the Federal Trade Commission's Identity Theft Victims' Complaint and Affidavit. It can be downloaded at *www.ftc.gov/ bcp/edu/resources/forms/affidavit.pdf*. You can also use the one in Appendix C of this book. Fill out the form and use it when communicating with the credit bureaus, account holders, credit grantors, collection agencies, or the police. You will need this report if you ever try to file an extended alert or freeze on your credit report.

TASK TWO:
GET HELP FROM LAW ENFORCEMENT

It is extremely important that you file a police report with your local police department. You'll find most of the people you talk to are a lot more cooperative if you can show that your local police, at least, take the theft seriously enough to assign it a case number. Some organizations, such as the credit bureaus, may refuse to take any action until you produce a police case number.

Before filing the police report, write out your own version of what happened. Be as detailed as you can, giving dates, times, names, and dollar amounts. If you're not completely sure that your identity has been stolen but think there's a good chance it has been, this is where you get to explain yourself. Whether you lost your wallet, your house was broken into, or your laptop was stolen, write it all down with as many details as you can.

When and if you're lucky enough to talk to a police officer in person, start by handing the officer a copy of your statement. It makes his or her job easier and saves you from inconsistencies caused by an inaccurate transcription of a verbal report.

Many large urban areas have automated systems you can use to report your theft. Many will also allow you to file the report in person. Try to do this if you can, because an officer who's experienced with identity theft can make sure you're following proper procedures.

The official police report is usually referred to as an Identity Theft Report. You may live in an area where the officer is not obligated to give you a copy. If this is the case, get one of the officer's business cards. Ask him or her to sign a statement (that you'll write) confirming that you have been the victim of identity theft and listing his or her badge number and your case number. If all else fails, print out the FTC affidavit you completed and try to get the officer to sign that. Remember: It will be very difficult for you to get a freeze or an extended fraud alert placed on your credit records if you don't have anything official to document your theft.

Some police departments are more cooperative about identity theft than others. Try a different jurisdiction if you run into a complete brick wall. Your county or state police may prove to be more helpful.

If you live in a small town or rural area, be prepared to explain to the police officer what you need and why. This may be the first time he or she has run into a case of identity theft.

You may want to file reports with other police departments as well. As you begin to monitor your credit reports, you may start to see patterns in the types of crimes the identity thief is committing. You might be able to identify activity in a specific geographic location, or the thief may be stupid enough to use a stolen credit card to pay for something traceable, like a rental car. In cases like these you should notify the local police in these jurisdictions and see if you can get them to take a report as well. The police have a much greater chance of tracing an identity thief if he or she is operating in their area.

Remember that police officers are human, too. Like most of us, they're a lot likelier to take an interest in your case if they have enough information to do their job properly. Do your homework, study the credit reports, and turn over any patterns you see to the police.

Remember that their jobs can be boring or frustrating much of the time and that all too often they're overworked. Don't make their jobs any harder. Just give them the facts clearly and without embellishment.

TASK THREE: START WORKING WITH THE CREDIT BUREAUS

Reporting your identity theft to the police may be an important first step and getting organized will make your task much easier, but learning how to work with the three major credit bureaus is where you can make the most difference in how successful you are in clearing your record.

Before going any further, you should understand a few things about how credit bureaus work. Regardless of their self-promotional advertising, these companies exist to serve businesses and NOT consumers—except in the sense that KFC serves chickens.

Essentially, a credit bureau (also referred to as a Consumer Reporting Agency or CRA) is a company that collects information about you and uses that information to provide a rating of your credit-worthiness. They collect this information from businesses that report on your ability to pay your bills. If you make your cell phone payments on time, Verizon will let the credit bureaus know. If you're late, Verizon will pass that information along as well.

The credit bureaus combine the reports they receive from businesses into a profile, or rating, of your overall ability to repay your debts. Businesses, in turn, use these credit ratings to determine, among other things, whether or not you should receive a mortgage and on what terms, what your credit limit should be, and whether to offer you new credit cards.

In a consumer-oriented society, credit-worthiness is a surrogate for trust. In a world where business is rarely done in person, the credit bureaus and their calculation of your credit-worthiness are the arbiters of your commercial reputation. As the use of these credit reports grows, the damage that incorrect information can do also grows proportionately.

A bad credit report can do more harm than just trigger a denial of credit. Many landlords run credit checks prior to renting houses or apartments and routinely deny leases to credit risks. Employers often use credit checks as part of the pre-employment screening process. Utility companies often conduct credit checks before they set up gas or electric accounts and will require a hefty cash deposit in lieu of a satisfactory report.

You will have difficulty getting a normal cell phone with a bad credit score. You will be unable to rent good hotel rooms and will find it almost impossible to rent a car. Even your sex life could suffer, as there are businesses that, for a fee, screen prospective matches for members of online dating services.

There are regulations that limit how negative information on credit reports can be used, but these laws are relatively weak. (See the following chapter for more details on this.) They generally put the burden on you to prove to the credit bureau and its clients why they should correct their reports.

This is one of the reasons why identity theft is so painful for the victim. The credit thief ruins your credit rating by taking money or goods from businesses and banks and making you responsible for repayment. In the process, they also complicate almost every aspect of your life—from buying a house or a car to getting a job and purchasing the things you need.

It's important for you to work with the credit companies to fix your files. The banks and business they work with are not necessarily eager to let you off the hook. You've got to produce good reasons for them to treat "your" debts differently and to adjust your credit record accordingly.

There are six basic steps involved in getting the credit bureaus to accept your point of view:

1. Get current copies of your credit reports.

There are three main CRAs: TransUnion, Equifax, and Experian. Their contact information is:

TransUnion

Fraud Victim Assistance Division
P.O. Box 6790, Fullerton, CA 92834-6790
Phone: 800-680-7289
E-mail (fraud victims only): *fvad@transunion.com*
Web: *www.transunion.com*

Equifax
P.O. Box 740250, Atlanta, GA 30374-0241
Phone: (888) 766-0008
Web: *www.equifax.com*

Experian
P.O. Box 9532, Allen, TX 75013
Phone: 888-EXPERIAN (888-397-3742)
Web: *www.experian.com*

Request a free report from each bureau at *www.annualcreditreport.com*, or by calling this organization, which is sponsored by the three CRAs, at 877-322-8228. (Do not request credit reports directly from the CRAs.) You'll want to get your "audit" of these credit reports underway quickly, so it's best to request them online if possible. If you order by phone it can take up to two weeks to get your copies.

2. Make a thorough inspection of the reports.

All credit reports have four (sometimes three) basic sections:

1. The *first section* is called the Credit Header and contains Personal Identifying Information (PII) such as your name, current address, employer, phone number, Social Security number, and date of birth.
2. The *second section* deals with your payment history and has a list of credit cards, banks, mortgages, co-signings, delinquencies, and collection histories. It reports each payment as either OK or delinquent and, if so, by how many days.
3. The *third section* lists public actions such as bankruptcies, judgments, and tax liens.
4. The *fourth section* lists credit inquiries, both yours and others.

Occasionally an account will be listed as in default or a "charge off." These entries can make it very difficult to get credit in the future.

Negative entries are usually placed at the top of the report right after the header.

As discussed in the previous chapter, entries that indicate fraudulent activity include:

Problems with your name or address in the Credit Header. An incorrect or additional address may indicate that an identity thief is having mail misdirected to gain access to account information, credit cards, etc.

In some cases the name or Social Security number may be wrong, while the rest of the report is correct. This may be the work of an identity thief creating a new "synthetic" identity from bits and pieces of several peoples' records.

New accounts that you didn't know about, credit inquiries from companies that you don't do business with, or credit inquiries from businesses in other geographical areas. These are clear signs that someone is attempting to defraud using your identity.

Denials of credit that you didn't know about or unknown new debts on existing accounts. This is an indication that an identity thief is already at work and has been for a while.

Once you've confirmed that your identity has been stolen and misused, your next step will be to report the fraud to the credit bureaus.

3. Notify the credit bureaus.

Notify the three credit bureaus that you are a victim of identity theft. (Notifying a single credit bureau should be sufficient as they are required by law to share the information, but you might want to make sure by notifying all three yourself.) Once notified, the bureaus will place an initial fraud hold on your account. This hold requires companies to contact you personally before they grant you any new credit, giving you some control over one of the worst aspects of the fraud.

Each of the credit bureaus should also send you a letter acknowledging your notification and assigning you a case number. Make a note of the case number and keep a copy in your files since you will need it in all future dealings with that CRA.

Setting the initial fraud alert on your credit reports also entitles you to another free credit report from each of the three bureaus. Take advantage of the offer. Remember that most identity thieves move quickly, and this may be your best opportunity to detect further fraud.

Unfortunately, this initial fraud alert only lasts ninety days. (Mark the end date on your calendar.) If you're lucky, the attempted fraud will turn out to be a one-time or one-incident event and you'll be able to resolve it within the ninety-day period. However, most consumers find the process takes longer. So your next step will be to try to extend the length of the initial fraud alert.

4. Try to extend the fraud alert.

If you can prove that there have been attempts to open fraudulent accounts in your name, you can try to convince the credit bureaus to extend their ninety-day fraud alert to seven years.

At this stage, you must communicate with all three credit bureaus separately and simultaneously. Do not assume that filing with one will alert the others.

The burden of proof is on you. In theory, the Identity Theft Report you received from the police should be enough to convince the CRAs. In practice, a police report is just the minimum level of documentation. You may also be asked to show further proof that your identity has actually been stolen, not just that you suspect it.

If the CRAs decide to question your filing for an extended hold (and they often do), they must request the additional information from you within fifteen days. They then have fifteen more days to work with you to get the information they need and then five more days to review that information.

If the CRAs agree to give you an extended fraud alert, would-be creditors are legally obligated to get your permission before they issue you credit for the next seven years. (It is up to you to make sure the extended alert doesn't somehow disappear from your credit reports during that time.) You are also entitled to two more free reports from each of the three agencies within the next twelve months.

Another benefit is that your name will be removed from the credit bureaus' direct marketing sales for the next five years. This will stop you from getting pre-approved credit offers that, if intercepted, can further complicate your situation. This is a profitable business for the bureaus, and they are understandably reluctant to remove you or anyone else from their lists, so you may have to remind them.

Because the two fraud alerts (initial and extended) stop thieves from opening new accounts, they can help you make sure that the damage to your credit doesn't spread. They will not help if any of your existing accounts are taken over (such as when you lose a credit card) and the overall level of protection they offer is weak at best since there's no law forcing prospective creditors to check your credit file. Companies that don't bother to check credit reports are perfectly free to grant "you" credit, and you can only hope that these offers don't find their way into the wrong hands.

(Note: Deployed military personnel who find themselves the victim of identity theft can also get a special "active duty military alert" which lasts for twelve months.)

5. Consider "freezing" your credit reports.

Most states (except for Alabama, Michigan, and Missouri) allow you to "freeze" your credit report. Four states (Arkansas, Kansas, Mississippi, and South Dakota) only provide freezes for victims of identity theft. A freeze is more effective than a fraud alert because it restricts access to your credit report. You can look at your file, but no one else can unless you lift the freeze, presumably preventing any new credit from being granted. Most states that offer this capability also allow the credit bureaus to charge a nominal fee for the privilege. Unfortunately, you will have to pay each of the three credit bureaus separately. If you do need to give someone access to your file, the freeze can usually be temporarily lifted by using a PIN or a password.

The biggest problem with credit freezes is that you will have to "thaw" the freeze when you want to get new credit. To do so, you'll need to know which of the three credit reporting bureaus the potential creditor uses.

Another limitation to credit freezes is that your credit can still be viewed by companies that you have an existing relationship with or collection agencies acting on their behalf. Under some circumstances, marketing companies attempting to prescreen consumers for new credit are also allowed to undo the freeze.

Check the Appendices of this book for specific details on your state's laws, and look at *www.consumersunion.org—003484indiv.html* or contact your state's consumer affairs department for updated and detailed information on your rights.

6. Correct your credit reports.

The final and most important step is to send the CRAs a dispute letter specifying any accounts or charges you believe are fraudulent and explaining why. Send it via certified mail as before, and include a copy of the FTC Identity Theft Affidavit you've filled out along with a copy of your police report.

The last page of each credit report is a dispute form for that particular credit bureau. Fill it out and attach copies of any supporting documentation to your correspondence. The form has several blocks that you can check off as "Paid in Full," "Account Closed," "Payment Never Late," etc. There is also an "Other" block where you can explain that an account was opened fraudulently or that charges were made by an unauthorized person.

Once you question part of the report, the credit bureau is obligated to investigate within thirty days. As a practical matter, they will check with the creditor who sent them the original entry. If the notifying party says it's accurate, you will be told that it has been investigated and found accurate. If it's wrong, the CRA should remove it from your credit report.

In fact, the credit providers use semi-automated processes rather than really investigating anything. They check the disputed item against their current database. If the reported problem is still there, the provider will report that it has "validated" the entry.

Because this process is so heavily stacked against consumers, your best bet is to contact the company that reported the problem directly. Again, send a letter explaining why the charges are fraudulent by certified mail, return receipt requested and include copies of the FTC affidavit and your police report. Get them to agree (in writing, if possible) to remove the information from their database. If the creditor agrees to do so, the credit bureaus are also required to remove the entry. (See Task Four below for more details on dealing with individual firms.)

If the company that reported the problem to the CRA doesn't agree with you and won't correct their database, you can have a 100-word statement placed on your credit report next to the negative information. Each of the credit bureaus has its own policies on what they will accept for comments, but it is best to just dispute the entry factually with details such as dates, account numbers, and amounts. A good comment might be something like: "account opened by unauthorized third party," or "charges after October 30th are fraudulent," or something similar.

If the creditor and the credit bureau stand by their original reports, you do not have a lot of recourse under the current law. You can send another note reciting the facts, providing supporting documentation, and politely insisting that they look at the information again. If they refuse, you may need to hire a lawyer familiar with FCRA issues. You can find lists of them at several places on the web or by asking your State Bar Association for referrals. There is an up-to-date list of lawyers specializing in these cases, as well as other useful contacts, at Mari Frank's identity theft website (*www.identitytheft.org*).

You can also try talking to your congressional representative or senator. A note on congressional stationery will usually get more attention than one coming directly from you. At the very least, you can be sure that a human being will actually look at it rather than leaving the process in the hands of automated software. You can also send a note to the FTC (*www.ftccomplaintassistant.gov*) that may help in the future, but is not likely to help you much right now.

Unfortunately, many consumers complete all of these steps, even convincing the creditor and the credit bureau to remove the information from their report, and then the same erroneous entry reappears on their credit report. It might be the fault of the credit provider, a subsidiary company, a collection agency, or the credit bureau itself. For this very reason it is absolutely necessary to get everything in writing. As soon as the incorrect entry reappears, you can drop the written evidence in the mail.

TASK FOUR:
START WORKING WITH SPECIFIC CREDITORS

If, during the scan of your credit reports in Task Three, you find new and unexplained accounts in your name, contact the businesses or financial organizations that provided the credit and close the accounts. Cancel any and all suspicious accounts. If in doubt, close it out. You can always reopen an account later. The companies will report your actions to the CRA, so ask them to report that the account was closed "at the customer's request." If, instead, they report that the account was closed due to a lost or stolen credit card, for example, your credit rating may suffer.

Call them to get the process started and try to get a good idea of how their process works, how it's different from the other companies you've dealt with, and what they need from you.

One of the most frustrating parts of this process will be finding the right person to talk to about your situation. Start by asking to speak to the company's fraud department. This should work with most credit card companies and banks, but you might have trouble finding a fraud department in the case of a small retail operation. Try to get a direct number so you don't have to go through the voice mail maze every time you call.

Try to make personal contact with whoever is on the other end of the line so they see you as a person and not a number. They might go the extra mile for you or at least give you honest advice instead of a runaround.

Always follow up in writing. Each company should get a written request to close any fraudulent accounts or to correct information that the creditor is reporting to the credit bureaus. Enclose copies of any documents that support your case, including letters from the credit bureaus and police reports. Send all such letters certified, return receipt requested, and put it in your file when you get the receipt/signature card back stapled to your copy of the letter that you sent.

Keep copies of all correspondence with the individual companies in your file. If you have a lot of correspondence with any one company, you may want to start a separate file for just that company. Whenever you communicate with a creditor, request they send you everything in their files documenting the fraudulent activity that occurred in your name. Add all of this to your file, and record any other communication in your notebook.

Some of the credit card companies will require you to fill out their own fraud reporting forms. It can be pretty frustrating to endlessly recopy your information onto a stack of customized forms, but you are much better off giving them what they want rather than arguing about the process. Keep your eye on your goal—protecting your finances and your credit.

It may be difficult, but try to maintain a positive attitude in all of your dealings with these companies. Getting angry, even though it's often justifiable usually ends up slowing down or stopping any progress you were making. A sense of humor also helps.

Your goal is to stop them from reporting negatives to the credit bureaus. Once they have a copy of the police report, they are obligated to stop reporting the problem, but not necessarily to remove any previous entries.

If bank accounts are involved, contact the bank, recording any and all conversations in your log. Close out the account, open a new one, and get new debit cards or checks. Consider putting stop payments on any outstanding checks even though you'll probably be charged a small fee for this.

It is usually much easier to resolve a problem with a company that you already do business with. They have files that show your correct address and history of charges and payments and will want to keep you as a customer.

EXTRA CREDIT: REPEAT AS NECESSARY

As mentioned earlier, just completing these tasks will NOT put an end to your problems; they can only begin to repair the damage done by the theft. You will have to continue monitoring your credit closely for at least two years. Request new credit reports as often as you feel necessary, and make sure to inspect them—and your bank and credit card statements—carefully for new problems. Don't forget to keep your files updated and available. You don't know when a new problem will arise, and you'll want to be able to respond quickly. If the police have succeeded in catching the person who committed the theft, you may be able to breathe a little easier, but keep in mind that identity thieves often sell their stolen information to others so it's entirely possible that your confidential information will still be compromised.

09.

LIMITS ON THE CREDIT INDUSTRY

It may seem like we're focusing too much on the credit bureaus, but I hope it's become obvious that they are key players when it comes to fixing identity thefts. In terms of your financial independence, they can play the role of prosecutor, judge, and jury. However, their power is not unlimited. Congress has passed a number of laws designed to protect consumers from credit reporting organizations. Here is a quick summary of the main statutes that cover their business:

THE FAIR CREDIT REPORTING ACT

Susan Brady's nerves were frazzled. She had been getting calls every night for the last few weeks from collection agencies trying to get paid for some debts that her ex-husband had rung up after they'd separated. Last night, a guy on the phone had said some pretty mean things to her, including telling her she was lowlife trash and that she'd be going to jail if she didn't pay. He also said that he was going to start calling her workplace and telling whoever answered the phone that she was a deadbeat.

But tonight Susan was ready for the call. After reading some books, she'd found out that she didn't have to put up with being talked to like that, that it was illegal to contact her at work or to keep calling her late at night, and that she probably wasn't responsible for the debt anyway. She couldn't wait for the call tonight. She was going to inform the caller that she had already notified the collection agency, in writing, that she no longer wanted to be contacted, and was rejecting responsibility for the debt.

Most of your rights related to credit reporting are contained in the Fair Credit Reporting Act. This law was created in 1970 to give you legal protection when you have to deal with credit reporting in general and identity theft in particular. The FCRA restricts the activities of consumer reporting agencies, including both the three national organizations as well as the smaller, special purpose entities that provide background checks for insurance companies, detective agencies, landlords, and employers.

The FCRA requires credit reporting bureaus to make your credit report available to you for a small fee, and to provide a free copy whenever action is taken against you as a result of the information they collect. These actions include termination of employment, denial of credit, or an increase in insurance costs. The FCRA also requires the CRAs to make credit reports more comprehensible, although they all still include "coded" information in their reports that only creditors will understand.

The FCRA also limits how credit reports can be used. As a practical matter, the uses permitted are so broad there are not many actual restrictions. A few of the permissible ones include credit applications, insurance matters, leases or rentals, employment screening, business account reviews, child support payments, compliance with court orders, and, of course, law enforcement. Prior to 9/11, law enforcement had to make an effort to get access to these reports. For example, the FBI was required to report their requests to Congress—albeit in aggregate form. Since the passing of the Patriot Act, these reporting requirements have been removed. Today you can assume that anyone working in national security has complete access to any and all credit reports.

It is also worth noting that credit bureaus are prohibited by law from telling a consumer that his or her record has been provided to a law enforcement agency.

The laws prohibit the release of medical information without your consent. (Although, again, national security matters probably over-rule this consideration.) You also have to consent to allow potential employers access to your reports, although most will demand permission in advance as a condition of employment. The law also protects consumers from the misuse of credit information. For example, there's a blanket prohibition against using medical data for determining credit-worthiness.

The law was designed to prevent the use of credit reports in targeted marketing campaigns. All three national bureaus, however, offer bulk data products to marketing organizations. Equifax and Experian are currently operating under a consent decree with the FTC on specifically this issue, and TransUnion has repeatedly challenged this restriction in court.

Other companies that are not actually credit reporting agencies are under no such restrictions and are perfectly free to sell credit data to anyone. Some of them, like Acxiom and Choicepoint, have created products that are sold to government agencies to circumvent legal restrictions preventing the government from collecting consumer information. In other words, the government can't collect this kind of data, but it can buy it.

The FCRA also makes it legal for consumers to dispute their credit reports. As explained in the previous chapter, the credit bureau is required to investigate challenges made by a consumer. If the original provider of the information determines that it is inaccurate, the CRA has thirty days to remove the information. If the information provider confirms that the information is correct, the information will stay on your credit record, but you have the right to add a short (100-word) disclaimer to be included on the credit report.

Perhaps most importantly, the FCRA provides a legal basis for consumers to sue credit bureaus, data furnishers, or certain other intermediaries such as a purchaser of a credit report. Suits can be brought in either federal or state court. Not only can you recover actual damages, but you can also receive court costs, legal fees, and even punitive damages. The FTC can also file criminal charges under the Act, although they would only do this in the case of widespread fraud.

This ability to sue is limited by a qualified immunity provision that protects credit bureaus from civil actions except where there's "malice or willful intent to injure." As you can imagine, this can be difficult to establish and, as a result, the right to sue isn't as powerful as it might be.

There's also a statute of limitations for filing a suit under the FCRA: two years from when you discover the violation but within five years of the actual date of the violation.

THE FAIR AND ACCURATE
CREDIT TRANSACTIONS ACT

The most important factor contained in credit reports is often not even visible: your credit score. Negative information—failure to pay, late payments, etc.—reported to the credit bureaus will almost always hurt your credit score and limit your ability to get credit.

The Fair and Accurate Credit Transactions Act of 2003 (FACTA) extends the rights covered in the FCRA to credit scores. The law requires CRAs, similar businesses, and mortgage companies to provide consumers their scores (for a fee) upon request.

The Act also entitles consumers to the free annual credit reports mentioned previously, and lets consumers opt out of so-called affiliate marketing, where the credit bureau provides personal information to an affiliated company to use in marketing programs.

FACTA amended the FCRA to hold the credit bureaus to a higher standard of investigation, that of "reasonable," and holds information providers to a higher standard concerning the accuracy of their reports. The act also requires credit providers to inform consumers if they are offered less than favorable credit terms as a result of their credit report.

FACTA also provided for the one call fraud alerts (where one call notifies all three bureaus), extended fraud alerts, and active duty military alerts.

If a creditor is notified by you that the debt that they're trying to collect is the result of identity theft, FACTA prohibits creditors from selling it or turning your debt over to a collection agency.

This is one of the keystone pieces of legislation that protects you if your identity is stolen.

THE FAIR DEBT COLLECTION PRACTICES ACT (FDCPA)

This 1978 statute provides consumers with some basic protections against unfair practices by debt collectors.

Under this Act debt collectors may *not*:

- Contact you at work if you ask them to stop
- Contact you outside normal hours (8 A.M. to 9 P.M. local time)
- Contact you at all if you notify them (in writing) to stop. There are exceptions: They can contact you to let you know if they're dropping the collection *or* initiating legal action.
- Publicly post your name or address as a debtor
- Claim that they are a lawyer (if they're not) or misrepresent themselves in any way to collect the debt by deceit
- Threaten arrest or any other impermissible act
- Swear at you or be otherwise abusive
- Communicate with any third party about your debt, other than your spouse or attorney

You can bring suit against a debt collector who violates the FDCPA and collect reasonable attorney fees and damages of up to $1,000.

DO CREDIT BUREAUS NEED MORE REGULATION?

In my opinion, the FCRA and FACTA do not go far enough. The wide variety of state laws that also cover credit reporting and collecting is a good indicator of this. Current laws are designed to protect the consumers, but the CRAs serve businesses first and tend to comply with legal requirements only grudgingly. Getting both a credit bureau and a credit card company to agree to remove a charge from a credit report often seems like pulling teeth. Even if you succeed, you have to do so three times, once for each CRA. Even then, the incorrect information often pops back up again at some future date.

Congress could solve some of these issues by making it even easier to sue the CRAs and increasing the amount of punitive damages. Also, there's absolutely no reason why every consumer shouldn't be allowed to look at all of their credit reports as many times as they want, for free, without having to prove that they have been the victims of identity theft.

PART III

HOW TO PROTECT YOUR IDENTITY

10.

KEEP YOUR IDENTITY SAFE

This is probably the most important part of this book. As we've seen, identity theft can be difficult to trace, difficult to diagnose, and even more difficult to remedy. Your best bet is to develop "safe identity" practices that help you avoid identity theft altogether. Threats to your security can come from many different directions and lead to many different kinds of results. It's often difficult to determine exactly what happened, and it can be nearly impossible to predict what will happen next.

BE PARANOID

Be skeptical, suspicious, and even a little paranoid when it comes to your identity. It's difficult to recognize threats in advance, and clever thieves make sure their attempts are carefully hidden.

The basic principle for protecting your identity is to reduce access to your personal information. This means reducing the number of people—and organizations—who have it. The fewer the companies possessing your information, the less likely it is that you will have your identity stolen.

What follows is a list of good general practices that you should use to build a "safe identity" shield.

You Don't Need to Share!

We're taught from the time we're little children how important it is to share our toys, our time, our attention, and our feelings with other people. One of the hardest parts of teaching people to protect themselves against identity theft is convincing them to fight their natural inclination to answer questions. Some people are willing to tell strangers their life story—including their account information and passwords—if they're asked politely. The problem is that we're not on the playground anymore. Some of the people asking questions about our personal information have no right to it. In fact, they want it because they want to see how many of our assets they can steal.

Anyone who asks for more personal information than they really need should be treated with caution. Being careful is not the same as being rude. Protecting your privacy is one of the most important aspects of defending against identity theft.

Refuse to Provide Personal Information Unless It's Really Necessary

Sometimes it seems as if everyone you talk to wants more information than they really need. Doctors and hospitals want Social Security numbers and have recently started insisting on making copies of driver's licenses. Many businesses try to get your phone number when they sell you something when it should be pretty clear that they don't really need it and that you don't automatically have to give it to them. Have any of them ever called you? Would you want them to? Nearly everyone asks for e-mail addresses these days—even the grocer and the dry cleaner!

In terms of identity theft, it's a good idea to challenge every request for unnecessary personal information. It's okay to push back a little. Ask whether they really need it and what they're going to use it for. Most businesses will back down on these requests if challenged since they don't want to alienate a regular or even a potential customer.

The risk of sharing your phone number may not be immediately apparent. Phone numbers help marketers solve a difficult data mining challenge: how to find unique values that help them manipulate large databases. There are probably a lot of John Smiths, many of whom buy batteries, but only one has the phone number 202-555-4567. This quest for unique values that allow marketers to target specific individuals drives this institutional snoopiness.

From a privacy perspective, you should try to avoid letting retailers get too much information on your purchasing habits. One of their most effective tools is the so-called "courtesy card." Supermarkets, drugstores, and mall chain stores all use them. You probably have a couple in your wallet that get you discounts and special pricing if you present these cards while shopping. This may seem like an easy way to save a couple of dollars on your weekly shopping bill, but think about how much your grocery and drug store purchases say about you. Marketing companies buy this data from the stores, link it up with the other information they have about you, and analyze it for marketing opportunities.

The more personal information on you that's out there, the more that's available to an identity thief. Don't think that you're protected because everyone has only a little piece of your information with no one having the whole perspective. Data-mining companies spend lots of money every year putting these little pieces together and selling the big picture to marketing companies. You don't have to make their job any easier.

Especially Your Social Security Number!

The best unique identifier of all, of course, is your Social Security number because it is the only number that every American has for life. This makes it an irresistible target—for both marketing companies and identity thieves.

Your Social Security number and some background information is all it takes to steal your identity. Government agencies use the SSN for authentication, and it's a requirement for getting new documents like passports, birth certificates, and driver's licenses. An SSN is all it takes to request a credit report, and it's often one of the main authentication items necessary to get access to your cell phone and bank accounts. Before identity theft became such a problem, you used to see SSNs used as identification for all kinds of business—in some cases they have even appeared on driver's licenses. Some businesses ask for your SSN as a matter of course. It may make you uncomfortable to refuse to provide it, but it just makes sense to keep it to yourself as part of an overall strategy of limiting access to your sensitive information.

Do Not Call Me!

Take advantage of the National Do Not Call registry offered by the federal government. Registering for this list prevents telemarketers from calling you. You can register your phone number(s) at *www. donotcall.gov*. There is a complaint form on the site; use it if you are harassed by telemarketers who don't scrub their list as they're supposed to. It does not prevent calls from businesses that you have an existing relationship with. (For that, see "opt out" below.) And, unfortunately, you're out of luck if you're being harassed by a political or charity fundraiser—both are exempt from these restrictions.

Many states offer similar programs. Some have combined their Do Not Call lists with the national program, but many still maintain their own. Listing at both the state and federal level may be a duplication of efforts, but it may also provide more reliable protection. Information about state programs is available from the Direct Marketing Association at *www.the-dma.org/government/donotcalllists.shtml*.

Read Privacy Policies

All commercial websites post privacy policies detailing what they will or will not do with your information. It's enlightening, if a little boring, to read these statements. They are usually written in dense legalese and are designed to keep the business from getting sued, no matter what. Most of them reserve the right to share your information with their "partners and associates"—which means pretty much anyone with whom they have a business relationship. These could be call centers in India, collection agencies, administrative workers, credit card number processors, collection agencies, or systems administrators.

Most also have a get-out-of-jail-free-type clause saying they can change their policy at any time—as long as they notify you, usually by posting it on their website. Lawyers limit their firm's privacy policies because the FTC has gone to court to stop companies from selling their customers' personal information if they said they wouldn't in a published policy.

Many banks and financial institutions are required by law to send their customers annual notices of their privacy policies. Most notices give you the option of "opting out" of the company's marketing efforts—and their sharing of your information with their "partners and associates"— by calling their customer service department or by mailing in a request. This may seem like a waste of time, but you have to weigh the value of your time against the potential risks. There's absolutely no way for you to judge whether the security policies of these organizations are adequate. Better to just stay off the list when you have the opportunity.

Opt Out

If you buy things online, you're often asked to check a little box to indicate that you're willing to let the company contact you or be included on their mailing list. This is known as "opting in." Naturally, they try to dress this up to make it sound exciting, saying that they will tell you about unannounced sales or special offers. If you shop with the company a lot, trust them, and know that they really do make special offers, go ahead and check the box. If you are not a regular customer, don't. Less reputable companies pre-check this box so you're automatically on their mailing list if you don't notice it or fail to uncheck it. The least reputable companies just ignore your choice and add you to their mailing list anyway.

I would guess that roughly half of all companies ignore your decision and just add you to their database anyway, but you should still make a point of opting out whenever you can. The fewer marketing databases you're in, the less likely it is that your identity will be stolen in a data breach. Keep in mind that your e-mail is also subject to the company's "partners and associates" sharing—so every time you do check the box it's more than likely you'll end up added to multiple databases.

Tell the Truth, But Only the Truth You Need to Tell

Only provide as much information as you really must. If you're buying something by credit card, for example, you only need to provide your name, address, and a valid credit card number. If you want a company to contact you with information or send you a receipt or shipping information, then you will have to give them a valid e-mail address.

In cases where a website requires more information than they really need, consider making something up. Many websites, especially those that offer only useful information like the weather or theater times, are designed to collect personal information. They try to get it by forcing you to create an account to access the site. Many daily newspapers, including the *Washington Post*, force you to register before they let you read an article. If you give them your authentic information, it will almost certainly end up in a marketing database. If you expect to go back to the website, fill the registration form with invented information and use that invented identity to access the site in the future. Personally, I like to register as literary figures or U.S. presidents.

Shred Your Documents

For about $100, you can get the single most useful weapon in your war against identity thieves—a paper shredder. All of us throw away reams of paperwork containing personal information. Dumpster diving identity thieves make their living by retrieving this information from your trash. At a minimum, you should destroy any document that contains your Social Security or financial account numbers, including credit card receipts from purchases. Keep a "shred box" in the room where you pay bills. When the box gets full, take a few minutes to shred it into unidentifiable confetti. Cross-cut shredders make it more difficult for persistent thieves to reassemble your paperwork, and high-end shredders will also cut up credit cards and magnetic media.

Keep Track of Your Credit Cards

Try to keep an eye on what happens when you hand your credit card to a clerk. If he or she disappears for an unusually long period of time, ask why. Make a mental note of the incident, and check for any unusual activity on the card in the future. Be even more suspicious if you're overseas—credit card theft can be almost impossible to trace or prosecute once you're back home.

Destroy all unwanted credit cards, either ones you're not using or ones that you received unsolicited. Cut them into pieces too small to be reassembled by an identity thief. Shut down any accounts that you no longer use. Checking your credit report is a good way to uncover these orphaned accounts. Not only do they detract from your credit-worthiness (potential creditors may count these unused credit lines against the total credit they feel you can carry) but, because you're clearly not paying attention to them, they're ripe for an identity thief. One good indicator that your identity has been stolen is seeing activity on these dormant accounts. The more you restrict your credit to accounts that you actually use, the less vulnerable you are.

Search Google for Your Name

One excellent way to see what's available on you publicly is to do what celebrities, politicians, and narcissists do routinely—search Google for your name! I've helped dozens of people search online for information about themselves and they are almost always shocked by what they find.

You may find samples of your college work (and possibly, your recreational activities) on the Internet. Comments on blogs, message boards, and forums never really go away. Reviews on Amazon or Yahoo! will be there forever. Public databases provide records of all of your political contributions, and real estate transactions are also a matter of public record. You can even find pictures of yourself online, even if you aren't aware of it—on someone else's Facebook page, for instance.

Even if you don't post information on yourself, others might do it for you. It's relatively simple to find our home addresses on the Internet and pretty easy to discover our job histories, our hobbies, and identify some of our family and friends. Over 50 percent of corporate Human Resources people admit to a Google search on potential employees as a screening tool.

After monitoring your credit report, knowing what information about you is available on the Internet is one of the most important steps you can take in protecting your identity. I recommend that you search Google for yourself at least once a month. If you do find information that would help an identity thief, you can either try to get it removed (always difficult on the Internet, where information tends to change every day, but lasts—somewhere—forever) or take other measures to protect yourself more rigorously.

Check Your Credit

Since we've already looked at credit bureaus in great detail, I'll try not to repeat too much information here. Still, inspecting and correcting your credit report on a regular basis is one of the most powerful tools you have in preventing identity theft. This requires two main actions on your part:

Monitor Your Credit Report

You can get a free report from each credit bureau annually by going to *www.annualcreditreport.com*, by calling toll-free 877-322-8228, or by completing the Annual Credit Report Request Form available at *www.ftc.gov/credit* and mailing it to: Annual Credit Report Request Service, P.O. Box 105281, Atlanta, GA 30348-5281.

By studying these annual reports in detail (as described a few chapters ago) you can detect any sign of fraud or abuse at the outset. This will limit the amount of damage thieves can do to you and may even help the police bring them to justice.

Correct Your Credit Report

This process is described in great detail in Chapter 8. Make sure to correct anything you see that is wrong or incomplete. The cleaner your credit report is, the more likely you'll be able to tell if something goes wrong.

A few additional services are available that can help you protect your credit.

Credit Monitoring Services

For an annual subscription fee these businesses monitor your credit reports for you and will notify you when something new pops up on your record.

Consumer advocacy groups and government agencies such as the FTC do not recommend these services. Most of them do what they say they'll do, but it isn't really much more than you can do yourself—and for free.

If you do decide that you'd like to use one of these services, check online and with the Better Business Bureau. Make sure that they have a good reputation and satisfied clients.

Credit Score Monitoring Services

The most prominent of these is called "MyFICO" and is run by FICO (formerly known as Fair, Isaac and Company), the business that generates the industry-leading credit score. They will notify you when your score changes—for a fee. Since the score only changes because of a modification in the underlying credit report, this offers you essentially the same service as the credit monitoring services. Each of the three credit bureaus offers similar credit monitoring products.

Identity Theft Insurance

Several insurance companies offer a service that will pay money for claims arising from identity theft. These policies range wildly in premiums, exemptions, and the extent to which they will pay. Most do not compensate you for indirect costs such as lost wages and opportunities. Some pay for legal services, and most at least partially pay to help fix fraudulent credit applied for in your name. If you're considering purchasing one of these policies, do your homework before you sign up.

Lawyers

Many lawyers advertise that they can help you fix identity theft and related credit problems. Few lawyers will take this kind of case on a contingency basis; almost all will require a steep fee.

It might make sense to engage a lawyer if your personal information was provably mishandled in violation of the law. In most normal identity theft cases, however, you can easily write the letters and file the documents yourself.

Lawyers can sometimes help by writing intimidating letters that look official, but most of the players in the credit business are used to these and have pretty good lawyers of their own.

One service that has gotten a lot of press lately is called LifeLock. They claim to protect your data by automatically renewing fraud alerts, opting out of pre-approval marketing lists, and monitoring hacker lists and address databases The company's advertising features LifeLock's CEO, Todd Davis, displaying his actual Social Security number. The implication is that he's so sure that his product works that he's willing to share his SSN with anyone.

The company claims that it will spend $1,000,000 to help members correct any problems caused by identity theft. There are many caveats in the fine print, and it should be noted that Mr. Davis himself has had his identity stolen on at least one occasion—and at least twenty people have applied for fake driver's licenses in his name.

STAY SAFE—ON YOUR COMPUTER AND ONLINE

Two-thirds of American households have a home computer, and yet only a small fraction of the population knows how to use these machines safely. Some of the most distressing incidents of identity theft happen through simple carelessness or ignorance of basic computer security. Here are a few ways to keep your computing safe and your identity intact.

Use Secure Passwords

Passwords are the front line in your battle against identity thieves. Make sure that you use passwords that are safe and secure and can withstand the attacks of online identity thieves.

It was easier to pick good passwords when you didn't need that many. Today, almost everyone who uses the Internet has to remember several, if dozens, of passwords. Most people pick something clever and easy to remember and use that same password everywhere, at least until it gets them into trouble.

The first problem with this approach is that there are free programs available on the Internet that can crack almost any password, given enough time. They work by trying a series of guesses based on a dictionary of common words. Experienced hackers also know that most people use similar methods of creating memorable passwords so they try those combinations first, such as variations of the user's name and birth date, family members, the college that they attended, etc. According to *PC Magazine*, the ten most common passwords are:

- password
- 123456
- qwerty
- abc123
- letmein

- monkey
- myspace1
- password1
- link182
- (your first name)

Other bad ones include every obvious obscenity and the words "secret" and "top secret."

The best way to formulate a password is to pick one that's unlikely to be discovered by the above methods. Never use anything personal (like a middle name) or obvious (like your birthday). Don't use numbers in any obvious sequence (like "12345"). Don't use strung-together dictionary words—they are susceptible to the dictionary attack. Always use at least 6 characters and make sure that they're a combination of letters and numbers. One popular trick is to take a real word and replace some of the letters with numbers, like "c0rv3tt3" instead of "corvette."

It's also important to use different passwords in different places. One of the first things a hacker will do with a successfully broken password is to try it at other popular sites that you might have used. If you've used it for all of your accounts, you may find yourself completely cleaned out.

If you do reuse passwords, be careful not to repeat one you've used for an important site—say, your bank account. Websites differ dramatically in how well they are secured, and it would be a shame if an identity thief was able to access your savings because you repeated the password you use to access your fantasy baseball league.

Password-Protect Your Hardware

Make sure to use passwords to protect your hardware as well as your software. Secure your iPods, cell phones, Wi-Fi routers and networks, etc. The more layers of security an identity thief has to crack to get at your information, the less likely he is to succeed. Network security is particularly important, so use the strongest you have available. Many home networking systems give you the choice of WEP or WPA—WPA is much safer.

Passwords and Encryption

Most good application programs like Word and Excel allow you to password-protect a file. Any file that you create that holds sensitive personal information should be protected in this way.

But password protection, even if it uses fingerprint recognition, does not completely protect your data. Once a malicious person has figured out or somehow circumvented your password, they will still be able to read and copy your information. An even better option is to combine password protection with encryption for really sensitive files. Consumer encryption products are just starting to come on to the market. For example, there are hard drives and thumb drives that automatically encrypt your data. There are also a number of good commercial software products, along with a few free open-source programs. If you password-protect your files, and the contents are also encrypted using a separate and different key, you can make an identity thief's life very difficult.

Pick Tough Challenge Questions

Many websites, in an attempt to be consumer friendly, offer you an alternative way to log in if you've forgotten your password. You'll be given a choice of "challenge" questions and answers when you first set up your account. If you can correctly answer the challenge questions, they'll give you access to your account. When you do set up this kind of account, make sure to use questions and answers that are as difficult to guess as possible. You can also improve the security of this process by not answering appropriately. If the site asks for your pet's name, for example, answer with the name of your hometown. This way even thieves who have access to your personal records will fail to pass the challenge authentication. Just make sure to make a note of your answer—or you may not be able to take advantage of this alternative when you need it.

Keep Your Passwords in a Safe Place

Where should you keep all of your passwords? If you keep your master list on your computer, PDA, or phone and you lose the device or a hacker is able to access it, you've lost everything. If you print out a list and tape it near your computer, you run the risk of a sneak thief finding and copying your list. There isn't a perfect answer to this question. In strictly security terms, any system of passwords depends on its weakest link. Your best choice is a method that you know you will use and can keep secure. A few commercial programs help solve the problem by encrypting the password list on your computer, but then they need to be locked and unlocked with a master password. One popular alternative is to keep your passwords in a little pocket notebook. If you lose it or someone steals it, of course, you're out of luck, but a single small notebook is usually pretty easy to hide and find when you need it.

Don't E-mail Sensitive Files

It's easy to get cavalier about digital information like e-mail or personal spreadsheets. We casually move them back and forth between home and work and often between desktops and laptops, sometimes even putting them on phones or PDAs. There are a lot of different ways to move these files: external hard drives, USB thumb drives, CDs, or, the easiest of all, e-mail.

E-mail is the most dangerous way to move sensitive files. Once you've sent it, copies of the e-mail, including attachments, are stored on your mail server. In most cases, you have no way of telling how secure the server is or who has access to it. Once the file is on the server, though, it can be almost impossible to secure it again. Anyone with access to the server can find and recover your e-mail. If you e-mail something to or from a work address, a copy of that e-mail will stay on the corporate server for quite a while, depending on the corporate data retention policy. Even once it's deleted it can usually be recovered from backups.

There's a good reason that almost every political scandal in the last twenty years has involved e-mail evidence. There's too much of it; we use electronic messages too casually. Incriminating e-mail has a bad habit of turning up at the wrong time. For instance, it's now routine for lawyers to subpoena e-mails in divorce cases.

If you do need to move sensitive information and files, you're much better off storing it on media, such as USB thumb drives, that are relatively easy to keep secure.

Be Careful with Suspicious Websites

It's fairly easy for anyone to download the pages of a website to his or her own computer. And any halfway competent programmer can use this material to create an impostor site that looks nearly as good as the original. There are a number of ways to make a fake URL appear real, and domain names aren't always what they seem to be. If you see anything that looks suspicious or wrong, trust your instincts.

For instance, *www.internationalbusinessmachines.com* is not run by the IBM Corporation and *www.whitehouse.com* was, for many years, a porn site. It's quite easy to create a URL that looks like it might be that of a well-known business but which isn't really related. If you're looking for the Disney movie studio, for example, should you look at *www.disney.com*, *www.walt_disney_studios.com*, *www.disneyworld.com*, or *www.disneystudios.com*?

Unless you're sure what the exact name is, you can easily be misled. As described in a previous section, an IP address is sometimes used instead of a domain name, as in *www.studios.192.168.1.1—disney*, which has nothing to do with the Disney Company. A good rule of thumb is the amount of time you spend validating a website should reflect the damage a phony site could cause.

Be Careful with Suspicious E-mails

E-mail addresses are nearly useless as a means of identification. First, anyone can pick any user name they want from most Internet service providers (ISPs), as long as it hasn't been taken yet. I can be *Johnny walker@myisp.com*, if the name is available, implying that my name (or my drink) is Johnny Walker—when it is not. It's also easy to spoof an e-mail address to make it look like mail is coming from someone else. What's not easy to do is to "catch" an e-mail aimed at someone else. That's why spoofed e-mails often change a field in the e-mail header so that any reply will be sent to someone other than the named sender. You can spot this by examining the long form of the e-mail headers (an option on all e-mail clients), although this is probably not the kind of thing you'd want to do on a regular basis.

Be Careful with Links in E-mails

When you get an e-mail that seems odd or is from a stranger or both, be very careful before you click on any links. There is a trick to reading links—ignore everything in the URL except for the part right before the .com, .org, or .net. If the address to the left of that dot is something unusual, DON'T click it. If you see a series of numbers or an IP address (four numbers ranging from 0 through 255, each separated by periods), don't click it. When in doubt, just don't click.

It's also important to realize that the address in the colored link in an e-mail is not necessarily the address that you will go to if you click on it. The way to determine this varies from mail reader to mail reader, but usually if you hover your cursor over the e-mail link, the underlying link will pop up. In some mail readers you can achieve the same effect by right-clicking the link.

Be Especially Careful When Downloading Files

Even if you are using antivirus software, you should still be careful about downloading anything from the Internet. Many people delight in collecting free programs that give weather reports, play Sudoku, or let you punch a monkey. Even if they're not malicious, these novelty programs will eventually slow your computer to a crawl. Most are harmless, but quite a few contain hidden software that can let scam artists take control of your computer. (File-sharing programs are notorious for this.) There are commercial solutions that prevent spyware from affecting your computer, but you're better off just limiting what you install.

Running programs within your browser is usually safe. However, you need to be extremely cautious if a window pops up and announces that a program wants to download a file, install a program, or run a script. If you are not 100 percent sure that the process is safe, just click the cancel button.

Create a Disposable E-mail Address

Consider opening up a free e-mail account at hotmail or gmail specifically for dealing with one-time visits to commercial websites. You'll get the information you need, although you won't be able to use the e-mail account for long: Your pristine account will be swamped with spam as soon as the retailer sells your address to direct marketers. Many ISPs allow you to have multiple e-mail addresses for one account. Save one for your commercial transactions and use the others for your regular e-mail. You'll be surprised how much less spam you'll get to your "everyday e-mail" address. Less spam is a good sign—it means that you're in fewer databases, and being in fewer databases means your information is less likely to be stolen.

Have as Few Online Accounts as Possible

When you buy something online, the retailer may invite you to open an account for your "shopping convenience." In most cases, the retailer only collects your e-mail address for receipts and shipping information. This can be annoying, as you end up on their marketing list, but it usually isn't dangerous.

Some sites, though, want to store your shipping and billing address and credit card information to make it more convenient for you to use the site in the future. These sites are often the targets of identity thieves, and it's impossible to know whether their security is good enough to protect your sensitive information. That's a lot of risk for a little bit of convenience.

The best approach is to routinely refuse to let retailers store your financial information. It's okay to make exceptions for sites that you trust and shop at frequently, but even then you should make sure to check your transaction history for unexplained purchases.

If you find that you've stopped using a popular site that you've stored your information at in the past, you can check to see if it's possible to remove the information. As with credit accounts, the fewer you have, the fewer opportunities thieves have to misappropriate your information.

Make Sure Your Information Is Completely Deleted

One of the ugly secrets of the digital world is that it's almost impossible to completely delete anything. Deleting a file on a computer can easily be undone—there are a number of programs, some free, that can do this. Remember that even if you've deleted an e-mail, it's usually still saved on your mail servers.

Some applications save copies automatically. Microsoft Word, for example, often saves different versions of the document you're working on. The program keeps track of all of the changes that have been made to a file, even those that have been deleted. It's almost too easy to send someone a document that contains all of these hidden revisions, making it possible for them to reconstruct prior versions of the document. I have seen this happen countless times, even in e-mails from lawyers, who really should know better.

Completely Remove Your Information from Old Computers and Hard Drives

Various studies have shown that about one half of all discarded computers still contain personal data on them. Old computers can contain e-mail archives—usually a treasure trove of personal data—as well as search and browsing histories, account numbers, banking information, and personal photographs. No matter how well you think you've cleaned the files off your old computer, it is extremely important that you make absolutely sure the data is gone.

Consumers are not the only ones who throw away computers well stocked with information; companies and even governments have frequently done the same thing. In 2008, Australia's Auditor General bought ten used government computers at auction. Four of them had sensitive information still on the hard drives—including tax file numbers, salaries, and addresses of government employees.

There are many ways to erase data on an old computer. Several commercial programs write zeroes all over the disk. These work, as does the simple and expedient practice of moving a powerful magnet over the disk's surface. But the only sure way is to use a simple tool that most of us own—a hammer. Remove the hard drives from a computer and smash them. By cracking and misaligning the disk surface, you render it completely unreadable. The same rule applies to CDs, USB thumb drives, and external hard disks.

Dispose of Unused Cell Phones and PDAs

When is a computer not a computer? When it's a cell phone or other handheld electronic device. Phones, PDAs (like Palm Pilots and Black-Berries), and MP3 players can hold lots of personal information. Some of it is kept on removable memory cards that should always be taken out before disposing of the device. Be especially careful with newer iPods like the Touch or the iPhone. It's easy to overlook the contents of these devices when you decide to get rid of them. Since most people won't take a hammer to their cell phone or iPod, at least make sure that you clear all data off of the devices before you give it away, donate it, or sell it. The iTunes store sells applications that claim to zero out an iPod's data.

When getting rid of cell phones, remember that some newer models have what's called a "SIM" card that uniquely identifies the phone. These SIM cards can also contain personal information, such as phone numbers and contact information. Take out and destroy the SIM card before you get rid of the phone—unless you're moving it to a new phone.

Don't keep old cell phones or PDAs around unless you're willing to keep them secure. By the time you get around to recycling your drawer full of old cell phones, you may forget just how much personal data they contain. As long as they're sitting around with data on them, they can be just as useful to an identity thief as a credit card receipt. There are charities that accept donations of used cell phones, so wipe your old phones clean and get them out of the house.

Be Very Careful When Using Public Computers

Computers are like toothbrushes—everybody should have their own, and they really shouldn't be shared.

If you use someone else's computer for something personal, like checking your e-mail, they can, if they're talented enough and so inclined, recover your browsing session and/or read your e-mail. Web browsers save histories of the sites that you've visited. Even when they don't, the temporary files that they create are usually around for a while before the system automatically deletes them.

One such type of file, called a "cookie," saves some of the data you enter when you visiting a website. It's not difficult to find new or changed cookie files on a computer and crack them open to take a look at what you've been typing. This is also true for work computers. Be extremely wary about typing personal information into a shared computer or a public computer like an Internet kiosk, a hotel room computer, or at an Internet café.

When you're done with an unfamiliar computer, log out of everything you've been using. Sign out of web-based e-mail, social networking sites, and instant messaging sessions. Exit the browser and clean up after yourself. Delete any files you've downloaded—either onto the desktop or into the file system. Empty the trash. See if the browser will let you delete the browsing history and the caches (where copies of some of the websites you've visited may be stored). Make sure the browser wasn't set to save passwords automatically. If it was, delete those as well.

If you needed to log on to use the computer (customary for most networked computers), make sure that you log out. Otherwise someone can come along, restart your session, and harvest your information.

If you're using a public computer, watch carefully to make sure no one is trying to read your account name or password over your shoulder. If the next user has deciphered your log-in information, all of your other attempts to protect your information will be wasted.

Even if you do all of this, keep in mind that a trained hacker can still recover session information on the computer from temporary files. You may even have been victimized by key-logging software—programs that memorize everything that you type, even passwords, and store it in a file for the hacker to retrieve later.

Keep Your Software Up-to-Date

Computer companies are usually one or two steps behind the hackers and identity thieves, but you should still download and install security patches for system software as soon as they come out. Software patches that fix computer vulnerabilities seem to come out every month or so. It can be difficult to keep up with them all, and sometimes they introduce new problems, but if you don't stay up-to-date, your computer is open to the most recent hacking discoveries of the computer community. Programs like Word and Excel also have security weaknesses and new security patches are released for them frequently. Keep up-to-date on these as well.

Update Your Virus Protection

Viruses are another of the dirty little secrets of computer security. The same programming skills that make computers such wonderful tools are often put to work finding ways to wreak havoc. Fortunately, there is also a very active and aggressive industry based on selling virus prevention and removal software. These companies are just a few steps behind the creative hackers and programmers trying to steal your information. The more up-to-date your software is, the less you have to fear from viruses and other malware that you might inadvertently download or install.

Know Who's Messing with Your Computer

The rule of thumb with computer security is that no precaution is good enough to stop someone who has physical access to a machine. It's too easy to put in a keystroke logger, change the root or system password, or punch some other hole in your computer's defenses. Never let anyone touch your computer unless you trust them, and try not to let anyone play with it when you're not around.

If you use outside paid technical help, make sure that they're reputable, have been in business for a while, and are insured or even bonded. Think of how easy it would be for a computer repair shop to make copies of the hard drive of every computer they service—without leaving a trace.

Many people, even many small businesses, rely on friends or employees for routine maintenance. If your computers hold sensitive information of any kind, make sure you know and trust and supervise these people. Many users with technical experience can't resist the temptation to explore the computers they're working on.

11.

THE FUTURE OF YOUR IDENTITY

Identity theft is a crime where the criminal is nearly always unknown and the victim can have a hard time proving his own identity. Kafka would be proud.

It's disheartening to realize that identity theft has only been a crime in this country for the last fifteen years. Before that it was viewed as an individual credit problem. It's only recently that the law accepted identity theft as a crime in and of itself.

This failure to recognize the changes that have taken place in technology, business, and criminal behavior is the main reason why dealing with identity theft is still so difficult.

If we can't get past this failure to adapt to the present situation, the future outlook for your identity may be even worse.

WHY IS THERE SO MUCH IDENTITY THEFT?

Identity theft continues to spread for reasons that are partly opportunistic, partly technological, and partly legislative.

The opportunistic part is easy to understand. Identity theft is a low-risk, moderate-reward crime that can be automated and conducted from off-shore locations. This makes prosecution nearly impossible, even if the crime is detected.

Our technology for collecting information, facilitated by our growing online infrastructure, has long since outstripped our ability to administrate the system. Both regulated and unregulated database companies collect information on consumers at a frenetic pace. When their efforts are combined with data sharing and data aggregation, our identity is now available, in practical terms, nearly everywhere to nearly everyone. As these integrated marketing and security databases continue to grow and proliferate, we are creating more and more opportunities for our data to be compromised.

Finally, our legal system is clearly skewed in favor of the database companies. Each time laws are enacted that protect consumers, powerful corporate lobbyists add loopholes big enough to weaken the net impact of the legislation. FCRA and FACTA were good starts, but are not nearly enough.

The situation will get worse unless we address all three of these factors. The opportunistic aspect is the hardest to control. The Internet has created so many new opportunities for misappropriating data that it may be, frankly, too late to put this particular genie back in its bottle.

NEW TECHNOLOGIES

We might be more successful developing better technological solutions to the problems. We need better forms of low-cost, unique, and un-spoofable identification. There are a few promising approaches in the works, but none is "ready for prime time" as of the writing of this book. Biometrics show promise; fingerprints and retina scans work well at airports and government facilities, but have not yet gotten inexpensive enough to push the technology down to the level of personal computers and home networks. I suspect that a workable mass-market solution will have to be based on hardware, not software. Every form of software identification, even those based on strong cryptography, eventually boils down to a password—and passwords can always be compromised.

A universal authentication scheme might be one solution. This would allow a consumer to use a single secure login for multiple websites. This has been tried by Microsoft (Passport) and is currently being played with by Yahoo! and Google (OpenID). This has both positive and negative possibilities: There's less chance that a password will be compromised, but if the password is discovered it will expose users to potential fraud across the Internet.

Since 9/11, there has been a great deal of discussion about creating a universal ID card for U.S. citizens. Law enforcement would like to see a national ID system because it would make it harder to forge IDs and easier to catch criminals. The cards would initially be used for in-person identification, although it stands to reason that such a system would be designed for other purposes such as online identification or as a replacement for SSNs in public records. The idea of a national ID is controversial. Whether or not you think they're a good idea depends on how much you trust the government to protect your privacy and not abuse the information placed in its trust.

I'd like to think that private sector incentives will lead to a success-ful solution for this problem. Anyone who can solve it stands to make a great deal of money over the next ten years.

LEGISLATIVE INITIATIVES

In a very basic way, the state of our computer security is primitive. We have developed elaborate firewalls and state-of-the-art encryption systems, but we have also allowed the concentration of sensitive infor-mation in relatively unprotected databases where even small mistakes can have catastrophic results. The best intentions and best practices of millions of computer users can be undone by one poorly paid white-collar office worker who loses a laptop full of personal information.

We are badly in need of new legislation at the national level that requires companies to maintain better security when dealing with our personal information. At the very least, they should be held to the same standard as government workers dealing with classified informa-tion, or health workers handling our medical records.

The identity theft problem cannot be solved until information security is vastly improved, and this is not something the database industry can be allowed to regulate on its own. Too many businesses have too much information for the public to trust that they'll all do the right thing, and too many companies are making too much money selling products based on our personal information to expect them to stop unless we regulate their business practices. If they are forced to provide adequate security for their computer systems, they might not be able to sell our personal information for the same profits they make today. From my point of view, this would be a very good thing—for everyone but the database companies.

INCREASE THE PUNISHMENTS FOR DATA BREACHES

The federal government needs to not just develop regulations protecting consumer privacy, but they also need to set their own house in order as well.

Consumers Union, the publisher of *Consumer Reports*, conducted an investigation of public data breaches and concluded that "government is among the biggest sources of ID leaks and that penalties for ID theft are rarely imposed on those who are negligent." They analyzed records of publicly reported data breaches compiled by the nonprofit Privacy Rights Clearinghouse and found that more than 230 security lapses by federal, state, and local governments from 2005 through mid-June 2008 had resulted in the loss or exposure of at least 44 million consumer records containing Social Security numbers, driver's license numbers, and other personal information.

It's becoming all too common to see corporations hemorrhage huge amounts of consumer information because of their inadequate computer security.

A good way to change this would be to impose penalties, $20 per consumer record exposed, for example, on companies that expose information. This would translate into fines of tens of millions of dollars for the worst offenders. Perhaps this is what it will take to convince database companies that it will be cheaper to adopt good security than to pay large fines.

This would be a major new expense for these companies, but at present the costs are absorbed by the individual consumers whose identities have been misappropriated as a result of these corporate breaches.

At some point, these companies need to recognize their responsibility for protecting the consumer information they are buying and selling.

In some ways, the situation calls for solutions like those the Environmental Protection Agency implemented to curtail the most egregious cases of pollution in the 1970s. The only way to get polluting companies in line was to hurt them with escalating fines; the mounting costs eventually drew the attention of their boards of directors and, ultimately, the wrath of the shareholders. Similar legislation could be developed to give companies incentives to prevent data breaches.

The main purpose of this book is to help you survive identity theft and protect yourself against identity theft in the future. Technologies and business practices are changing so quickly that it's nearly impossible to make meaningful or useful predictions about the future of identity theft. As discussed earlier, your best response is to take security seriously, pay attention to warnings, stay up-to-date on new developments in the field, and keep your eyes open and alert for the new problems that you'll face in the future.

Appendix A

BASIC RESOURCES

Surprisingly, given just how big a problem identity theft has become, there are a limited number of organizations dedicated to assisting its victims. Below I have listed some of the most important. Many of these organizations are less concerned with supporting victims than they are with advocating changes in laws concerned with privacy and identity theft. Still, they will be useful resources to you in your campaign to clear your reputation and prevent future thefts of your identity.

The Identity Theft Resource Center (*www.idtheftcenter.org*)
This is a nonprofit organization devoted to educating the public about the dangers of identity theft. They offer victim support and consumer counseling, as well as resources for presentations, local community events, and information on law enforcement resources that are available to you if you've been the victim of identity theft. They also publish a regular newsletter.

The Federal Trade Commission (*www.ftc.gov*) (To make a complaint, use *www.ftccomplaintassistant.gov.*)
In addition to problems with identity theft, the FTC handles issues regarding bad business practices. Filing complaints with them can result in government action, including the prosecution of wrongdoers. On their site you can fill out a voluntary complaint form that will be filed with the agency.

The Federal Bureau of Investigation's (FBI) Internet Crime Complaint Center (*www.ic3.gov—default.aspx*)

This is a partnership between the FBI, the National White Collar Crime Center, and the Bureau of Justice Assistance. The center is specifically focused on cybercrime, so identity theft is only one of many illegal activities it pursues. You can make your complaint online, whether you yourself are the victim or you believe someone else to have been the victim of identity theft.

Electronic Privacy Information Center (EPIC) (*www.epic.org*)

EPIC is a public interest research group located in Washington, D.C. Its activities are focused on protecting free speech and the First Amendment. It publishes an online newsletter, "The EPIC Alert." Its relevance to identity theft victims lies in its focus on privacy issues that directly affect you if your identity is stolen. At the same time, EPIC doesn't offer resources aimed directly at identity theft victims, so you're better off turning elsewhere for immediate action.

Identity Theft: Prevention and Survival (*www.identitytheft.org*)

This site is run by Mari Frank, a California attorney who has written books on identity theft and sells CDs containing sample letters. Her site also contains links to other sites that provide services for identity theft victims.

Consumers Union (*www.consumersunion.org*)

Consumers Union is probably the most important consumer rights advocacy group in the United States. It includes resources on all types of consumer fraud, including identity theft. It conducts campaigns in favor of consumer-friendly legislation and publishes the influential magazine *Consumer Reports*. However, it has little on identity theft that you won't find elsewhere.

The Privacy Rights Clearinghouse (*www.privacyrights.org/identity.htm*) This is another nonprofit consumer information and advocacy organization. Their site includes identity theft fact sheets and quizzes, victims' stories, and links to other sites and publications.

Appendix B

THE FTC'S IDENTITY THEFT VICTIMS' STATEMENT OF RIGHTS

Source: *www.ftc.gov/bcp/edu/microsites/idtheft/consumers/rights.html*

This is an important document for you to know and understand, since it provides a summary of your rights under federal law as a victim of identity theft. If you have determined someone has stolen your identity, read this statement and, if you have questions, contact your state's attorney general.

IDENTITY THEFT VICTIMS' STATEMENT OF RIGHTS

Several federal laws protect victims of identity theft. These laws have to do with documenting the theft; dealing with credit reporting companies; dealing with creditors, debt collectors, and merchants; and limiting your financial losses caused by the theft of your identity. Here is a brief summary of the rights of identity theft victims, with links to websites that provide more information.

Documenting the Theft

You have the right to:

File a report with a law enforcement agency and ask for a copy of it to show how your identity has been misused. This report is often called a police report.

An identity theft report is a second kind of report. It is a police report with more detail. To be an identity theft report, it should have enough information about the crime that the credit reporting companies and the businesses involved can verify that you're a victim, and know which accounts or information have been affected. It's the report that will give you access to many of the rights described here.

The FTC's ID theft complaint form is a good place to start documenting the theft of your identity. This form asks you for the kind of detail that the identity theft report requires. Once you fill out this form online and print it, you can use it with the police report to create your identity theft report.

Dealing with Credit Reporting Companies
You have the right to:

Place a 90-day initial fraud alert on your credit files. You would do this if you think you are—or may become—the victim of identity theft. A fraud alert tells users of your credit report that they must take reasonable steps to verify who is applying for credit in your name. To place a 90-day fraud alert, contact just one of the three nationwide credit reporting companies. The one you contact has to notify the other two.

Place a seven-year extended fraud alert on your credit files. You would do this if you know you are a victim of identity theft. You will need to give an identity theft report to each of the credit reporting companies. Each credit reporting company will ask you to give them some way for potential creditors to reach you, like a phone number. They will place this contact information on the extended fraud alert as a signal to those who use your credit report that they must contact you before they can issue credit in your name.

Get one free copy of your credit report and a summary of your rights from each credit reporting company. You can get these when you place a 90-day initial fraud alert on your credit reports. When you place an extended fraud alert with any credit reporting company, you have the right to two copies of that credit report during a 12-month period. These credit reports are in addition to the free credit report that all consumers are entitled to each year.

Ask the credit reporting companies to block fraudulent information from appearing on your credit report. To do this, you must submit a copy of a valid identity theft report. The credit reporting companies then must tell any creditors who gave them fraudulent information that it resulted from identity theft. The creditors may not then turn the fraudulent debts over to debt collectors.

Dispute fraudulent or inaccurate information on your credit report with a credit reporting company. The credit reporting company must investigate your charges, and fix your report if they find that the information is fraudulent.

In many states, you have the right to restrict access to your credit report through a credit freeze. A credit freeze makes it more difficult for an identity thief to open a new account in your name. Your state attorney general's office has information about using a credit freeze where you live.

Dealing with Creditors, Debt Collectors, and Merchants

You have the right to:

Have a credit report free of fraudulent accounts. Once you give creditors and debt collectors a copy of a valid identity theft report, they may not report fraudulent accounts to the credit reporting companies.

Get copies of documents related to the theft of your identity—for example, applications used to open new accounts or transaction records—if you give the company a valid police report. You also can tell the company to give the documents to a specific law enforcement agency; that agency doesn't have to get a subpoena for the records.

Stop the collection of fraudulent debts. You may ask debt collectors to stop contacting you to collect on fraudulent debts. You also may ask them to give you information related to the debt, like the names of the creditors and the amounts of the debts.

In many states, you have the right to be notified by a business or organization that has lost or misplaced certain types of personal information. Contact your state attorney general's office for more information.

LIMITING YOUR LOSS FROM IDENTITY THEFT

Various laws limit your liability for fraudulent debts caused by identity theft.

Fraudulent Credit Card Charges: You cannot be held liable for more than $50 for fraudulent purchases made with your credit card, as long as you let the credit card company know within 60 days of when the credit card statement with the fraudulent charges was sent to you. Some credit card issuers say cardholders who are victims of fraudulent transactions on their accounts have no liability for them at all.

Lost or Stolen ATM/Debit Card: If your ATM or debit card is lost or stolen, you may not be held liable for more than $50 for the misuse of your card, as long as you notify the bank or credit union within two business days after you realize the card is missing. If you do not report the loss of your card promptly, your liability may increase.

Fraudulent Electronic Withdrawals: If fraudulent electronic withdrawals are made from your bank or credit union account, and your ATM or debit card has not been lost or stolen, you are not liable, as long as you notify the bank or credit union in writing of the error within 60 days of the date the bank or credit union account statement with the fraudulent withdrawals was sent to you.

Fraudulent Checks: Under most state laws, you are liable for just a limited amount for fraudulent checks issued on your bank or credit union account, as long as you notify the bank or credit union promptly. Contact your state banking or consumer protection agency for more information.

Fraudulent New Accounts: Under most state laws, you are not liable for any debt incurred on fraudulent accounts opened in your name and without your permission. Contact your state attorney general's office for more information.

OTHER FEDERAL RIGHTS

Identity theft victims have other rights when the identity thief is being prosecuted in federal court. For example, under the Justice for All Act, the U.S. Department of Justice says identity theft victims have the right:

- To be reasonably protected from the accused
- To reasonable, accurate, and timely notice of any public court proceeding, any parole proceeding involving the crime, or any release or escape of the accused
- To not be excluded from any such public court proceeding unless the court determines that the identity theft victim's testimony would be materially altered if he or she heard other testimony at that proceeding
- To be reasonably heard at any public proceeding in the district court involving release, plea, sentencing, or any parole proceeding

- To confer with the attorney for the government in the case
- To full and timely restitution as provided in law
- To proceedings free from unreasonable delay
- To be treated with fairness and with respect for his or her dignity and privacy

OTHER STATE RIGHTS

You may have additional rights under state laws. Contact your state attorney general's office to learn more.

Appendix C

THE FTC'S MODEL LETTER FOR REPORTING IDENTITY THEFT

> Downloadable PDF available at:
> *www.ftc.gov/bcp/edu/resources/forms/affidavit.pdf*

You don't have to follow this letter exactly, but it's a useful form for making sure you're giving authorities what they need to know in order to pursue those who've stolen your identity. Even if you decide not to send this letter in the form found online, I recommend you fill it out so you have all the information you'll need in a readily accessible format. Keep a copy of the letter with your information in your Identity Theft File.

INSTRUCTIONS FOR COMPLETING THE ID THEFT AFFIDAVIT

To make certain that you do not become responsible for any debts incurred by an identity thief, you must prove to each of the companies where accounts were opened in your name that you didn't create the debt. The ID Theft Affidavit was developed by a group of credit grantors, consumer advocates, and attorneys at the Federal Trade Commission (FTC) for this purpose. Importantly, this affidavit is only for use where a new account was opened in your name. If someone made unauthorized charges to an existing account, call the company for instructions.

While many companies accept this affidavit, others require that you submit more or different forms. Before you send the affidavit, contact each company to find out if they accept it. If they do not accept the ID Theft Affidavit, ask them what information and/or documentation they require.

You may not need the ID Theft Affidavit to absolve you of debt resulting from identity theft if you obtain an Identity Theft Report. We suggest you consider obtaining an Identity Theft Report where a new account was opened in your name. An Identity Theft Report can be used to (1) permanently block fraudulent information from appearing on your credit report; (2) ensure that debts do not reappear on your credit reports; (3) prevent a company from continuing to collect debts or selling the debt to others for collection; and (4) obtain an extended fraud alert.

The ID Theft Affidavit may be required by a company in order for you to obtain applications or other transaction records related to the theft of your identity. These records may help you prove that you are a victim. For example, you may be able to show that the signature on an application is not yours. These documents also may contain information about the identity thief that is valuable to law enforcement.

This affidavit has two parts:

Part One—the ID Theft Affidavit—is where you report general information about yourself and the theft.

Part Two—the Fraudulent Account Statement—is where you describe the fraudulent account(s) opened in your name.

Use a separate Fraudulent Account Statement for each company you need to write to.

When you send the affidavit to the companies, attach copies (NOT originals) of any supporting documents (for example, driver's license or police report). Before submitting your affidavit, review the disputed account(s) with family members or friends who may have information about the account(s) or access to them.

Complete this affidavit as soon as possible. Many creditors ask that you send it within two weeks. Delays on your part could slow the investigation. Be as accurate and complete as possible. You may choose not to provide some of the information requested. However, incorrect or incomplete information will slow the process of investigating your claim and absolving the debt. Print clearly.

When you have finished completing the affidavit, mail a copy to each creditor, bank, or company that provided the thief with the unauthorized credit, goods, or services you describe. Attach a copy of the Fraudulent Account Statement with information only on accounts opened at the institution to which you are sending the packet, as well as any other supporting documentation you are able to provide.

Send the appropriate documents to each company by certified mail, return receipt requested, so you can prove that it was received. The companies will review your claim and send you a written response telling you the outcome of their investigation. Keep a copy of everything you submit.

If you are unable to complete the affidavit, a legal guardian or someone with power of attorney may complete it for you. Except as noted, the information you provide will be used only by the company to process your affidavit, investigate the events you report, and help stop further fraud. If this affidavit is requested in a lawsuit, the company might have to provide it to the requesting party. Completing this affidavit does not guarantee that the identity thief will be prosecuted or that the debt will be cleared.

If you haven't already done so, report the fraud to the following organizations:

1. **Any one of the nationwide consumer reporting companies to place a fraud alert on your credit report.** Fraud alerts can help prevent an identity thief from opening any

more accounts in your name. The company you call is required to contact the other two, which will place an alert on their versions of your report, too.

Equifax: 800-525-6285; *www.equifax.com*
Experian: 888-EXPERIAN (397-3742); *www.experian.com*
TransUnion: 800-680-7289; *www.transunion.com*

In addition, once you have placed a fraud alert, you're entitled to order one free credit report from each of the three consumer reporting companies, and, if you ask, they will display only the last four digits of your Social Security number on your credit reports.

2. **The security or fraud department of each company where you know, or believe, accounts have been tampered with or opened fraudulently.** Close the accounts. Follow up in writing, and include copies (NOT originals) of supporting documents. It's important to notify credit card companies and banks in writing. Send your letters by certified mail, return receipt requested, so you can document what the company received and when. Keep a file of your correspondence and enclosures.

When you open new accounts, use new Personal Identification Numbers (PINs) and passwords. Avoid using easily available information like your mother's maiden name, your birth date, the last four digits of your Social Security number, your phone number, or a series of consecutive numbers.

3. **Your local police or the police in the community where the identity theft took place.** Provide a copy of your ID Theft Complaint filed with the FTC (see below), to be incorporated into the police report. Get a copy of the police report or, at the very least, the number of the report. It can help you deal with creditors who need proof of the crime. If the police are reluctant to take your report, ask to file a "Miscellaneous Incidents" report, or try another jurisdiction, like your state police. You

also can check with your state attorney general's office to find out if state law requires the police to take reports for identity theft. Check the Blue Pages of your telephone directory for the phone number or check *www.naag.org* for a list of state attorneys general.

4. **The Federal Trade Commission.** By sharing your identity theft complaint with the FTC, you will provide important information that can help law enforcement officials across the nation track down identity thieves and stop them. The FTC also can refer victims' complaints to other government agencies and companies for further action, as well as investigate companies for violations of laws that the FTC enforces. You can file a complaint online at *www.consumer.gov—idtheft*. If you don't have Internet access, call the FTC's Identity Theft Hotline, toll-free: 877-IDTHEFT (438-4338); TTY: 866-653-4261; or write: Identity Theft Clearinghouse, Federal Trade Commission, 600 Pennsylvania Avenue, NW, Washington, DC 20580.

When you file an ID Theft Complaint with the FTC online, you will be given the option to print a copy of your ID Theft Complaint. You should bring a copy of the printed ID Theft Complaint with you to the police to be incorporated into your police report. The ID Theft Complaint, in conjunction with the police report, can create an Identity Theft Report that will help you recover more quickly. The ID Theft Complaint provides the supporting details necessary for an Identity Theft Report, which go beyond the details of a typical police report. Do not send the affidavit to the FTC or any other government agency.

The Federal Trade Commission's model letter for reporting identity theft appears on the following pages.

ID THEFT AFFIDAVIT

(1) My full legal name is:

_____

(2) (If different from above) When the events described in this affidavit took place, I was known as:

_____

(3) My date of birth is:

_____

(4) My Social Security number is:

_____

(5) My driver's license or identification card state and number is:

_____

(6) My current address is:

_____

_____
city   state   zip code

(7) I have lived at this address since: _____
(month/year)

(8) (If different from above) When the events described in this affidavit took place, my address was:

_____

_____
city   state   zip code

(9) I lived at the address in Item 8 from _____ to _____
(month/year)   (month/year)

(10) My daytime telephone number is: (_____) _____

My evening telephone number is: (_____) _____

Check all that apply for items 11–16:

(11) ❑ I did not authorize anyone to use my name or personal information to seek the money, credit, loans, goods, or services described in this report.

(12) ❑ I did not receive any benefit, money, goods, or services as a result of the events described in this report.

(13) ❑ My identification documents (for example, credit cards; birth certificate; driver's license; Social Security card; etc.) were stolen or lost on or about:

_____

(day/month/year)

(14) ❑ To the best of my knowledge and belief, the following person(s) used my information (for example, my name, address, date of birth, existing account numbers, Social Security number, mother's maiden name, etc.) or identification documents to get money, credit, loans, goods, or services without my knowledge or authorization:

_____   _____
name (if known)   *name (if known)*

_____   _____
address (if known)   *address (if known)*

_____   _____
address (if known)   *address (if known)*

_____   _____
phone number(s) (if known)   *phone number(s) (if known)*

Additional information (if known):

_____

_____

_____

_____

_____

_____

(15) ❑ I do NOT know who used my information or identification documents to get money, credit, loans, goods, or services without my knowledge or authorization.

(16) ❑ Additional comments: (For example, description of the fraud, which documents or information were used, or how the identity thief gained access to your information. Attach additional pages as necessary.)

_____

_____

_____

_____

_____

_____

_____

_____

_____

_____

_____

_____

_____

_____

_____

_____

_____

_____

_____

_____

_____

_____

_____

Appendix D

SAMPLE DISPUTE LETTER AND FOLLOW-UP LETTER

This template may be used to send disputes to the credit-reporting companies. Note that you should always be friendly and respectful in these letters—the reader will be an employee who receives hundreds of letters a day. Rudeness will only make them care less about you, and it won't help your case in court. Finally, keep your letters extremely brief and on topic. If you want to provide a long explanation, do so with a separate attachment.

Include a photocopy of your credit report and any supporting materials—never send originals. Mark them with identifying information (like "Exhibit A" and "Item #1") to make the process as easy as possible for the credit-reporting company, and to protect your rights.

SAMPLE DISPUTE LETTER

[DATE]

TO: *[CREDIT-REPORTING COMPANY]*
[ADDRESS OF CREDIT-REPORTING COMPANY]

Greetings:

Please correct the following errors on my credit report (a photocopy of the report, marked "Exhibit A," is enclosed with this letter). I'm disputing the following items:

> **Account:** ABC Credit Card Company, account #123456 (Exhibit A, Item #1)
> **Reason for dispute:** I never paid late. Please remove the late-payment notation.
> **Note:** Exhibit B shows on-time payments for every month.

> **Account:** Big Bank Auto Loan, account #987654 (Exhibit A, Item #2)
> **Reason for dispute:** This is not my account. Please do not report it with my history.
> **Note:** I do not live in Hawaii, and I never have.

Please investigate and correct these items promptly. Contact me in writing at the address below if you need further information from me. Please send a copy of these disputed items to the creditors listed above. If you will not send them this information, please inform me of that promptly.

Thank you for your help in this matter.

Sincerely,

[YOUR SIGNATURE HERE]
[YOUR FULL NAME]
[YOUR MAILING ADDRESS]
[YOUR SOCIAL SECURITY NUMBER]
[YOUR DATE OF BIRTH]
[YOUR PREVIOUS ADDRESSES IN THE PAST FIVE YEARS]

SAMPLE FOLLOW-UP LETTER

[DATE]

TO: [CREDIT-REPORTING COMPANY]
[ADDRESS OF CREDIT-REPORTING COMPANY]

Greetings:

I sent a dispute letter to your company on [DATE]. Because you have not responded to me within thirty days of receiving my request, my dispute must have been valid (Exhibit A shows a photocopy of that letter, and Exhibit B confirms when you received the letter via mail).

Please confirm that you have corrected the account listed below, and include a copy of my updated credit report. Please be sure that the disputed item does not reappear on my credit report.

Account: Big Bank Auto Loan, account #987654

Thank you for your help in this matter.

Sincerely,

[YOUR SIGNATURE HERE]
[YOUR FULL NAME]
[YOUR MAILING ADDRESS]
[YOUR SOCIAL SECURITY NUMBER]
[YOUR DATE OF BIRTH]

Appendix E

STATE RESOURCES

SECURITY FREEZE LAWS

One of the most important things to determine if you think you're a victim of identity theft is the status of your state's security freeze laws. As mentioned earlier, since many credit bureaus are providing inadequate protection for victims of identity theft, state governments have taken matters into their own hands. In a number of states, they have passed laws that allow consumers to "lock" or freeze their credit reports, preventing credit from being granted in their names. Once your freeze kicks in, potential lenders, creditors, employers, or anyone else will be unable to view your credit reports.

The information that follows, from Consumersunion.com, is valid as of September 2008. Be sure to check the Internet for the most updated status of your state's credit freeze laws.

Alabama

Alabama is one of the few states that has not passed a law requiring the availability of the security freeze. However, as of November 1, 2007, Equifax, Experian, and TransUnion are all making the freeze available voluntarily to Alabama residents. In order to effectively freeze access to your credit files, you must request the security freeze at all three major credit bureaus.

Eligibility: All consumers

Fees: No fee for identity theft victims. All others pay $10 to place, temporarily lift, or remove the freeze altogether.

Alaska

Eligibility: All consumers

Fees: No fees for identity theft victims with a copy of a complaint to law enforcement. All others pay a $5 fee to place the freeze and $2 for a temporary lift.

Effective date of law: July 1, 2009

Permanent freeze remains until removal requested by consumer.

Arizona

Security freeze rights established by state law.

Eligibility: All consumers

Fees: No fees for identity theft victims with police reports. All others pay a $5 fee to place the freeze, lift it temporarily, or remove it altogether. There is also a $5 PIN replacement fee.

Effective date of law: August 31, 2008

Arkansas

Security freeze rights for identity theft victims established by state law. All others use the voluntary program.

Fees: $10 to place the freeze, lift it temporarily, or remove it altogether.

Effective date of law: January 1, 2008

Permanent freeze remains until removal requested by consumer.

California

Security freeze rights established by state law.

Eligibility: All consumers

Fees: No fee for identity theft victims. All others pay $10 to place, temporarily lift, or remove the freeze; $12 fee to temporarily lift the freeze for a specific creditor.

Effective date of law: January 1, 2003

Permanent freeze remains until removal requested by consumer.

Colorado

Security freeze rights established by state law.

Eligibility: All consumers

Fees: No fee for the first freeze; $10 to lift the freeze temporarily or to remove it altogether. $12 to temporarily lift the freeze for a specific creditor. $10 to place a second freeze.

Effective date of law: July 1, 2006

Permanent freeze remains until removal requested by consumer.

Connecticut

Security freeze rights established by state law.

Eligibility: All consumers

Fees: $10 to place the freeze, lift it temporarily, or remove it altogether; $12 to lift it temporarily for a specific creditor.

Effective date of law: January 1, 2006

Permanent freeze remains until removal requested by consumer.

Delaware

Security freeze rights established by state law.

Eligibility: All consumers

Fees: No fee for identity theft victims. All others pay $20 to place the freeze, but no fees to lift it temporarily or remove it altogether.

Effective date of law: September 28, 2006

Permanent freeze remains until removal requested by consumer.

District of Columbia

Security freeze rights established by D.C. law.

Eligibility: All consumers

Fees: No fees for identity theft victims. All others pay $10 to place the freeze, but no fees to lift it temporarily or remove it altogether.

Effective date of law: July 1, 2007

Permanent freeze remains until removal requested by consumer.

Florida

Security freeze rights established by state law.

Eligibility: All consumers

Fees: No fees for identity theft victims and seniors 65 years and older. All others pay $10 to place the freeze, lift it temporarily, or remove it altogether.

Effective date of law: July 1, 2006

Permanent freeze remains until removal requested by consumer.

Georgia

Security freeze rights established by state law.

Fees: No fees for identity theft victims with police reports. No fee for placement of the freeze for seniors 65 or older. All others pay a $3 fee to place the freeze, lift it temporarily, or remove it altogether.

Effective date of law: August 1, 2008

Permanent freeze remains until removal requested by consumer.

Hawaii

Security freeze rights established by state law.

Eligibility: All consumers

Fees: No fees for identity theft victims. All others pay $5 to place the freeze, lift it temporarily, or remove it altogether.

Effective date of law: Original law limited to identity theft victims was effective January 1, 2007. All consumers became eligible for the security freeze on June 15, 2007.

Permanent freeze remains until removal requested by consumer.

Idaho

Security freeze rights established by state law.

Eligibility: All consumers

Fees: No fees for identity theft victims with police reports. All others pay a $6 fee to place the freeze, lift it temporarily, or remove it altogether. There is also a $10 PIN replacement fee.

Effective date of law: July 1, 2008

Permanent freeze remains until removal requested by consumer.

Illinois

Security freeze rights established by state law.

Eligibility: All consumers

Fees: No fees for identity theft victims with police reports and seniors 65 years and older. All others pay a $10 fee to place the freeze, lift it temporarily, or remove it altogether.

Effective date of law: January 1, 2007

Permanent freeze remains until removal requested by consumer.

Indiana

Security freeze rights established by state law.

Eligibility: All consumers

Fees: No fee to place the freeze, lift it temporarily, or remove it altogether.

Effective date of law: September 1, 2007

Permanent freeze remains until removal requested by consumer.

Iowa

Security freeze rights established by state law.

Eligibility: All consumers

Fees: No fee for identity theft victims. All others pay $10 to place the freeze, $12 to temporarily lift, or $10 to remove the freeze altogether.

Effective date of law: July 1, 2008.

Permanent freeze remains until removal requested by consumer.

Kansas

Security freeze rights established by state law.

Eligibility: Identity theft victims only. As of November 1, 2007, the security freeze will be offered by all three major credit bureaus voluntarily to all consumers.

Fees: No fees permitted by law for identity theft victims. All others pay $10 to place, temporarily lift, or remove the freeze altogether.

Effective date of law: January 1, 2007

Permanent freeze remains until removal requested by consumer.

Non-ID theft victims may use the voluntary program.

Kentucky

Security freeze rights established by state law.

Eligibility: All consumers

Fees: No fees for identity theft victims who provide a police report. All others pay $10 to place the freeze, lift it temporarily, or remove it altogether. $10 to have PIN reissued.

Effective date of law: July 11, 2006

Note: Security freeze automatically expires after 7 years from date of placement.

Louisiana

Security freeze rights established by state law.

Eligibility: All consumers

Fees: No fees for identity theft victims or persons aged 62 years and older. All others pay $10 to place the freeze or $8 to lift it temporarily. No fee to remove the freeze altogether.

Effective date of law: July 1, 2005

Permanent freeze remains until removal requested by consumer.

Maine

Security freeze rights established by state law.

Eligibility: All consumers

Fees: No fees for identity theft victims who provide a police report. All others pay up to $10 to place the freeze, lift it temporarily, or remove it altogether. $10 to have PIN reissued, and $12 to lift the freeze temporarily for a specific creditor.

Effective date of law: February 1, 2006

Permanent freeze remains until removal requested by consumer.

Maryland

Security freeze rights established by state law.

Eligibility: All consumers

Fees: No fees for identity theft victims who provide report of alleged identity fraud or with an identity theft report. All others pay $5 to place the freeze, lift it temporarily, or remove it altogether.

Effective date of law: January 1, 2008

Permanent freeze remains until removal requested by consumer.

Massachusetts

Security freeze rights established by state law.

Eligibility: All consumers

Fees: No fee for identity theft victims or victims' spouses. $5 to place the freeze, lift it temporarily, or remove it altogether.

Effective date of law: February 3, 2008

Permanent freeze remains until removal requested by consumer.

Michigan

Michigan is one of the few states that has not passed a law requiring the availability of the security freeze. Michigan consumers may use the voluntary program.

Eligibility: All consumers

Fees: No fee for identity theft victims. All others pay $10 to place, temporarily lift, or remove the freeze altogether.

Minnesota

Security freeze rights established by state law.

Eligibility: All consumers

Fees: No fees for identity theft victims who provide a police report. All others pay $5 to place the freeze, lift it temporarily, or remove it altogether.

Effective date of law: August 1, 2006

Permanent freeze remains until removal requested by consumer.

Mississippi

Security freeze rights for identity theft victims established by state law.

Eligibility: Identity theft victims with a police report, investigative report, or complaint filed with a law enforcement agency.

Fees: $10 to place a freeze for identity theft victims. All others pay $10 to place, temporarily lift, or remove the freeze altogether.

Effective date of law: July 1, 2007

Permanent freeze remains until removal requested by consumer. Non-ID theft victims may use the voluntary program.

Missouri

Missouri is one of the few states that has not passed a law requiring the availability of the security freeze. Consumers may use the voluntary program.

Eligibility: All consumers

Fees: No fee for identity theft victims. All others pay $10 to place, temporarily lift, or remove the freeze altogether.

Montana

Security freeze rights established by state law.

Eligibility: All consumers

Fees: No fees for identity theft victims. All others pay $3 to place the freeze or to lift it temporarily. $5 to have PIN reissued. No fee to remove the freeze altogether.

Effective date of law: July 1, 2007

Nebraska

Security freeze rights established by state law.

Eligibility: All consumers

Fees: No fees for identity theft victims and minors. All others pay a one-time $15 fee to place the freeze. No fee for lifting the freeze temporarily or removing it altogether.

Effective date of law: September 1, 2007

Note: Security freeze automatically expires after 7 years from date of placement.

Nevada

Security freeze rights established by state law.

Eligibility: All consumers

Fees: No fees for identity theft victims who submit a police report. All others pay $15 to place the freeze, $18 to lift it temporarily or remove it altogether. There is a $20 fee to lift it temporarily for a specific creditor.

Effective date of law: October 1, 2005

Permanent freeze remains until removal requested by consumer.

New Hampshire

Security freeze rights established by state law.

Eligibility: All consumers

Fees: No fees for identity theft victims who submit a copy of a police report, investigative report, or complaint to a law enforcement agency. All others pay $10 to place the freeze, lift it temporarily, or remove it altogether.

Effective date of the law: January 1, 2007

New Jersey

Security freeze rights established by state law.

Eligibility: All consumers

Fees: No fee to place the first security freeze. $5 fee to lift the freeze temporarily, remove it altogether, or to have PIN reissued.

Note: Consumers are also permitted to make such requests directly to consumer reporting agencies via secured electronic mail.

Effective date of law: January 1, 2006

Permanent freeze remains until removal requested by consumer.

New Mexico

Security freeze rights established by state law.

Eligibility: All consumers

Fees: No fees for identity theft victims with a copy of police or investigative report or for residents over 65 years of age. All others pay $10 to place a freeze and $5 to lift it temporarily or remove it altogether.

Effective date of law: July 1, 2007

Permanent freeze remains until removal requested by consumer.

New York

Security freeze rights established by state law.

Eligibility: All consumers

Fees: No fees for identity theft victims. All others can place the freeze for free the first time it is used. These consumers pay $5 to lift it temporarily or remove it altogether. If they wish to re-start the freeze after it is removed, they pay a $5 fee.

Effective date of law: November 1, 2006

Permanent freeze remains until removal requested by consumer.

North Carolina

Security freeze rights established by state law.

Eligibility: All consumers

Fees: No fees for identity theft victims with a valid report or complaint with a law enforcement agency. All others pay $10 to place the freeze, lift it temporarily, or remove it altogether.

Effective date of law: December 1, 2005

Permanent freeze remains until removal requested by consumer.

North Dakota

Security freeze rights established by state law.

Eligibility: All consumers

Fees: No fees for identity theft victims with a valid copy of a police report or police case number documenting the investigative report or complaint to law enforcement agency. All others pay $5 to place or lift the freeze. No fee for removing freeze.

Effective date of law: July 1, 2007

Ohio

Security freeze rights established by state law.

Eligibility: All consumers

Fees: No fee for identity theft victims. All others pay $5 to place the freeze, temporarily lift, or remove the freeze altogether.

Effective date of law: September 1, 2008, for the security freeze provisions.

Permanent freeze remains until removal requested by consumer.

Oklahoma

Security freeze rights established by state law.

Eligibility: All consumers

Fees: No fees for identity theft victims with investigative report or for seniors aged 65 years and older. All others pay $10 to place the freeze, lift it temporarily, or remove it altogether.

Effective date of law: January 1, 2007

Permanent freeze remains until removal requested by consumer.

Oregon

Security freeze rights established by state law.

Eligibility: All consumers

Fees: No fee for identity theft victims. $10 to place the freeze, lift it temporarily, or remove it altogether.

Effective date of law: October 1, 2007

Permanent freeze remains until removal requested by consumer.

Pennsylvania

Security freeze rights established by state law.

Eligibility: All consumers

Fees: No fees for identity theft victims or seniors aged 65 and older. All others pay $10 to place the freeze or to lift it temporarily. No fee to remove the freeze.

Note: Security freeze automatically expires after 7 years from date of placement.

Effective date of law: January 1, 2007

Rhode Island

Security freeze rights established by state law.

Eligibility: All consumers

Fees: No fees for identity theft victims or seniors aged 65 years and older. All others pay $10 to place the freeze, lift it temporarily, or remove it altogether.

Effective date of law: January 1, 2007

Permanent freeze remains until removal requested by consumer.

South Carolina

Security freeze rights established by state law.

Eligibility: All consumers

Fees: None.

Effective date of law: December 31, 2008

Permanent freeze remains until removal requested by consumer.

Until December 31, 2008, you may use the voluntary program.

South Dakota

Security freeze rights for identity theft victims established by state law.

Eligibility: Identity theft victims with a valid police report. As of November 1, 2007, the security freeze will be offered by all three major credit bureaus voluntarily to all consumers.

Fees: No fees permitted by law for identity theft victims. All others pay $10 to place, temporarily lift, or remove the freeze altogether. Note: Only freezes credit report and automatically expires after 7 years from date of placement.

Effective date of law: July 1, 2006

Tennessee

Security freeze rights established by state law.

Eligibility: All consumers

Fees: No fees for identity theft victims. All others pay $7.50 to place the freeze, no fee to lift it temporarily, and $5 to remove it altogether.

Effective date of the law: January 1, 2008

Permanent freeze remains until removal requested by consumer.

Texas

Security freeze rights established by state law.

Eligibility: All consumers

Fees: No fees for identity theft victims. All other consumers pay $10 to place the freeze, lift it temporarily, or to remove it altogether. There is a $12 fee to lift the freeze temporarily for a specific creditor.

Effective date of law: September 1, 2003 for identity theft victims; September 1, 2007 for all consumers

Permanent freeze remains until removal requested by consumer.

Utah

Security freeze rights established by state law.
Eligibility: All consumers
Fees: Utah's law allows credit bureaus to charge "reasonable fees," without specifying the amount that can be charged.
Note: Consumers will be able to temporarily lift or "thaw" the freeze within 15 minutes of electronic request.
Effective date of law: September 1, 2008
Permanent freeze remains until removal requested by consumer.

Vermont

Security freeze rights established by state law.
Eligibility: All consumers
Fees: No fees for identity theft victims. All others pay $10 to place the freeze and $5 to lift it temporarily or remove it altogether.
Effective date of law: July 1, 2006
Permanent freeze remains until removal requested by consumer.

Virginia

Eligibility: All consumers
Fees: No fees for identity theft victims with police reports. All others pay a $10 fee to place the freeze.
Effective date of law: July 1, 2008
Permanent freeze remains until removal requested by consumer.

Washington

Security freeze rights established by state law.
Eligibility: Originally applied to identity theft victims, including persons who received a notice of a security breach of computerized personal information. Beginning September 1, 2008, all consumers will be eligible for the freeze.
Fees: Consumers pay $10 to place the freeze, lift it temporarily, or remove it altogether.

Effective date of law: July 24, 2005 for identity theft victims; September 1, 2008 for all consumers

Permanent freeze remains until removal requested by consumer.

West Virginia

Security freeze rights established by state law.

Eligibility: All consumers

Fees: No fees for identity theft victims. All others pay $5 to place the freeze, lift it temporarily, or remove it altogether.

Effective date of the law: July 2, 2007

Permanent freeze remains until removal requested by consumer.

Wisconsin

Security freeze rights established by state law.

Eligibility: All consumers

Fees: No fee for an "individual who submits evidence satisfactory to the CRAs that the individual made a report to a law enforcement agency." All others pay $10 to place, temporarily lift, or remove the freeze altogether.

Effective date of law: January 1, 2007

Permanent freeze remains until removal requested by consumer.

Wyoming

Security freeze rights established by state law.

Eligibility: All consumers

Fees: No fees for identity theft victims. All others pay $10 to place the freeze, lift it temporarily, or remove it altogether.

Note: Requires electronic and telephone methods to lift; imposes 15 minute lift timeframe starting September 1, 2008.

Effective date of law: July 1, 2007

Permanent freeze remains until removal requested by consumer.

STATE GOVERNMENT
CONSUMER PROTECTION OFFICES

Following is a list of the offices in each state to which you can go for assistance if you're the victim of identity theft. The state office may refer you to a regional or city office for further action. Be sure to fully document your interaction with the personnel in these offices and, if you've reported the theft to the police, provide them with a case number and the names and badge numbers of any officers you've spoken to. Have a copy of your affidavit of identity theft (see p. 130) handy so you can supply them with the necessary information. Remember that these offices handle thousands upon thousands of complaints and questions each year, so the more detailed and documented the information you provide to them, the better the chances that they can help you.

Alabama

County Offices
Consumer Affairs Section
Office of the Attorney General
11 South Union St.
Montgomery, AL 36130
334-242-7335
Toll free: 800-392-5658 (AL)
Fax: 334-242-2433
www.ago.state.al.us

Alaska

Consumer Protection Unit
Office of the Attorney General
1031 West 4th Ave., Suite 200
Anchorage, AK 99501-5903
907-269-5100
Toll free: 888-576-2529
Fax: 907-276-8554
www.law.state.ak.us

Arizona
Consumer Protection and Advocacy Section
Office of the Attorney General
1275 West Washington St.
Phoenix, AZ 85007
602-542-5025
602-542-5763 (Consumer Information and Complaints)
Toll free: 800-352-8431 (AZ)
Fax: 602-542-4085
www.azag.gov

Consumer Protection
Office of the Attorney General
400 West Congress South Bldg., Suite 315
Tucson, AZ 85701
520-628-6504
Toll free: 800-352-8431 (AZ)
Fax: 520-628-6530
E-mail: *consumerinfo@azag.gov*
www.azag.gov

Arkansas
State Offices
Consumer Protection Division
Office of the Attorney General
323 Center St., Suite 200
Little Rock, AR 72201
501-682-2007
501-682-2341 (Consumer Hotline)
Toll free: 800-482-8982 (Consumer Hotline)
Toll free: 800-448-3014 (Crime Victims Hotline)
Toll free: 888-382-1222 (Do Not Call Program)
TTY: 501-682-6073
Fax: 501-682-8118 (Consumer Division)
E-mail: *oag@arkansasag.gov*
www.arkansasag.gov

California
California Department of Consumer Affairs
1625 North Market Blvd.
Sacramento, CA 95834
Toll free: 800-952-5210 (CA)
TTY: 916-322-1700; Toll Free: 800-326-2297
E-mail: *dca@dca.ca.gov*
www.dca.ca.gov

Office of the Attorney General
Public Inquiry Unit
PO Box 944255
Sacramento, CA 94244-2550
916-322-3360
Toll free: 800-952-5225 (CA)
TTY: 916-324-5564
Fax: 916-323-5341
E-mail: *piu@doj.ca.gov*
www.caag.state.ca.us

Colorado
Consumer Protection Division
Colorado Attorney General's Office
1525 Sherman St., 7th Floor
Denver, CO 80203-1760
303-866-5079
Toll free: 800-222-4444
Fax: 303-866-4916
www.ago.state.co.us

AARP ElderWatch
A program with the Colorado Attorney General and the AARP Foundation that fights elder financial abuse and fraud through information, education, referrals, and consumer advocacy.
1301 Pennsylvania #280
Denver, CO 80203
303-222-4444 option 2
Toll free: 800-222-4444 option 2
Fax: 303-831-6217
E-mail: *aarpelderwatch@aarp.org*
www.aarpelderwatch.org

Connecticut
Department of Consumer Protection
165 Capitol Ave.
Hartford, CT 06106
860-713-6050
Fax: 860-713-7243
www.ct.gov/dcp

Delaware
Fraud and Consumer Protection Division
Office of the Attorney General
Carvel State Office Building
820 North French St.
Wilmington, DE 19801
302-577-8600
Toll free: 800-220-5424
Fax: 302-577-6499
E-mail: *consumer.protection@state.de.us*
www.attorneygeneral.delaware.gov

District of Columbia
Office of Consumer Protection
Office of the Attorney General for the District of Columbia
941 N. Capitol Street NE
Washington, DC 20002
202-442-4615
Fax: 202-478-9296
www.dcra.dc.gov

Department of Consumer and Regulatory Affairs
Government of the District of Columbia
941 North Capitol St., NE
Washington, DC 20002
202-442-4400
202-727-1000 (Citywide Call Center)
Fax: 202-442-9445
E-mail: *dcra@dc.gov*
www.dcra.dc.gov

Office of Consumer Protection
Department of Consumer & Regulatory Affairs
941 N Capitol Street NE
Washington, DC 20002
202-442-4400
202-442-4615
Fax: 202-478-9296
www.dcra.dc.gov

Florida
Economic Crimes Division
Office of the Attorney General
PL-01 The Capitol
Tallahassee, FL 32399-1050
850-414-3600
Toll free: 866-966-7226 (FL)
TTY: 800-955-8771 (Toll free)
Fax: 850-488-4483
myfloridalegal.com

Multi-State Litigation and Intergovernmental Affairs
Office of the Attorney General
PL-01 The Capitol
Tallahassee, FL 32399-1050
850-414-3300
Toll free: 866-966-7226 (FL)
TTY: 800-955-8771 (Toll free)
Fax: 850-410-1630
myfloridalegal.com

Florida Dept. of Agriculture and Consumer Services
Division of Consumer Services
2005 Apalachee Parkway
Tallahassee, FL 32301
850-488-2221
Toll free: 800-435-7352 (FL)
Fax: 850-410-3839
www.800helpfla.com

Georgia
Governor's Office of Consumer Affairs
2 Martin Luther King, Jr. Dr., Ste. 356
Atlanta, GA 30334
404-656-3790
Toll free: 800-869-1123 (GA and outside Atlanta)
Fax: 404-651-9018
consumer.georgia.gov

Hawaii
Office of Consumer Protection
Department of Commerce and Consumer Affairs
345 Kekuanaoa St., Room 12
Hilo, HI 96720
808-933-0910
Fax: 808-933-8845
www.hawaii.gov/dcca

Office of Consumer Protection
Department of Commerce and Consumer Affairs
235 South Beretania St., Room 801
Honolulu, HI 96813-2419
808-586-2636
Fax: 808-586-2640
www.hawaii.gov/ocp

Office of Consumer Protection
Dept of Commerce and Consumer Affairs
1063 Lower Main St., Ste C-216
Wailuku, HI 96793
808-984-8244
Fax: 808-243-5807
www.hawaii.gov/ocp

Idaho
Consumer Protection Division
Idaho Attorney General's Office
650 West State St.
Boise, ID 83720-0010
208-334-2424
Toll free: 800-432-3545 (ID)
Fax: 208-334-4151
www.ag.idaho.gov

Illinois
Consumer Fraud Bureau
1001 East Main St.
Carbondale, IL 62901
618-529-6400
Toll free: 800-243-0607 (Hotline)
TTY: Toll free 877-785-9339 (IL)
Fax: 618-529-6416
E-mail: *ag_consumer@atg.state.il.us*
www.illinoisattorneygeneral.gov

Consumer Fraud Bureau
100 West Randolph, 12th Floor
Chicago, IL 60601
312-814-3000
Toll free: 800-386-5438 (IL)
TTY: 312-814-3374
Fax: 312-814-2549
E-mail: *ag_consumer@atg.state.il.us*
www.illinoisattorneygeneral.gov

Governor's Office of Citizens Action
222 South College, Room 106
Springfield, IL 62706
217-782-0244
Toll free: 800-642-3112 (IL)
Fax: 217-524-4049
E-mail: *governor@illinois.gov*
www.illinois.gov

Indiana
Consumer Protection Division
Office of the Attorney General
Indiana Government Center South
302 West Washington St.
Indianapolis, IN 46204
317-232-6330
Toll free: 800-382-5516 (Consumer Hotline)
Fax: 317-232-4393
www.indianaconsumer.com

Iowa

Consumer Protection Division
Office of the Iowa Attorney General
1305 East Walnut St., 2nd Floor
Hoover Building
Des Moines, IA 50319
515-281-5926
Toll free: 888-777-4590 (IA)
Fax: 515-281-6771
E-mail: *consumer@iowa.gov*
www.IowaAttorneyGeneral.org

Kansas

Consumer Protection & Antitrust Division
Office of the Attorney General
120 SW 10th, 2nd Floor
Topeka, KS 66612-1597
785-296-3751
Toll free: 800-432-2310 (KS)
TTY: 785-291-3767
Fax: 785-291-3699
E-mail: *cprotect@ksag.org*
www.ksag.org

Kentucky

Office of Consumer Protection
Office of the Attorney General
1024 Capital Center Dr., Suite 200
Frankfort, KY 40601
502-696-5389
Toll free: 888-432-9257 (KY)
Fax: 502-573-8317
E-mail: *attorney.general@ag.ky.gov*
www.ag.ky.gov

Kentucky Office of the Attorney General
Consumer Protection Division
1024 Capital Center Drive Frankfort, KY 40601
8911 Shelbyville Road
Louisville, KY 40222
502-696-5389
502-429-7134 (Jefferson County)
Toll free: 888-432-9257
Fax: 502-429-7129
E-mail: *decker@ag.ky.gov*

Louisiana
Consumer Protection Section
Office of the Attorney General
PO Box 94005
Baton Rouge, LA 70804-9005
225-326-6400
Toll free: 800-351-4889
Fax: 225-326-6499
www.ag.state.la.us

Maine
Bureau of Consumer Credit Protection
35 State House Station
Augusta, ME 04333-0035
207-624-8527
Toll free: 800-332-8529 (ME)
TTY: 888-577-6690 (Toll free)
Fax: 207-582-7699
www.credit.maine.gov

Consumer Protection Division
Office of the Attorney General
6 State House Station
Augusta, ME 04333
207-626-8800
Toll free: 800-436-2131 (Consumer Protection)
Fax: 207-626-8812
E-mail: *consumer.mediation@maine.gov*
www.maine.gov/ag

Maryland
Consumer Protection Division
Office of the Attorney General
200 Saint Paul Place, 16th Floor
Baltimore, MD 21202-2021
410-528-8662 (Consumer Complaints)
410-576-6550 (Consumer Information)
410-528-1840 (Health Advocacy unit)
Toll free: 888-743-0023
Toll free: 877-261-8807 (Health Advocacy unit)
TTY: 410-576-6372 (MD)
Fax: 410-576-7040
E-mail: *consumer@oag.state.md.us*
www.oag.state.md.us/consumer

Massachusetts
Executive Office of Consumer Affairs and Business Regulation
10 Park Plaza, Suite 5170
Boston, MA 02116
617-973-8700 (General Information)
617-973-8787 (Consumer Hotline)
Toll free: 888-283-3757 (MA)
TTY: 617-973-8790
Fax: 617-973-8798
E-mail: *consumer@state.ma.us*
www.mass.gov

Consumer Protection and Antitrust Division
Office of the Attorney General
One Ashburton Place
Boston, MA 02108
617-727-8400 (Consumer Hotline)
TTY: 617-727-4765
Fax: 617-727-3265
www.mass.gov/ago

Michigan
Office of Attorney General
Consumer Protection Division
PO Box 30213
Lansing, MI 48909
517-373-1140
Toll free: 877-765-8388
Fax: 517-241-3771
www.michigan.gov/ag

Minnesota
Consumer Services Division
Attorney General's Office
1400 Bremer Tower
445 Minnesota St.
St. Paul, MN 55101
651-296-3353
Toll free: 800-657-3787
TTY: 651-297-7206 or 800-366-4812 (Toll free)
Fax: 651-282-2155
E-mail: *attorney.general@state.mn.us*
www.ag.state.mn.us

Mississippi

Consumer Protection Division
Attorney General's Office
PO Box 22947
Jackson, MS 39225-2947
601-359-4230
Toll free: 800-281-4418 (MS)
Fax: 601-359-4231
www.ago.state.ms.us

Bureau of Regulatory Services
Department of Agriculture and Commerce
121 North Jefferson St.
PO Box 1609
Jackson, MS 39201
601-359-1111
Fax: 601-359-1175
www.mdac.state.ms.us

Missouri

Consumer Protection Division
Missouri Attorney General's Office
PO Box 899
Jefferson City, MO 65102
573-751-3321
Toll free: 800-392-8222 (MO)
TTY: 800-729-8668 (MO)
Fax: 573-751-7948
E-mail: *consumer@ago.mo.gov*
www.ago.mo.gov

Montana
State Offices
Montana Office of Consumer Protection
Department of Justice
2225 11th Avenue
PO Box 200151
Helena, MT 59620-0151
406-444-4500
Toll free: 800-481-6896
Fax: 406-444-9680
www.doj.mt.gov/consumer

Nebraska
Office of the Attorney General
Department of Justice
2115 State Capitol
PO Box 98920
Lincoln, NE 68509
402-471-2682
402-471-3891 (Spanish)
Toll free: 800-727-6432 (NE)
Toll free: 888-850-7555 (NE—Spanish)
Fax: 402-471-0006
www.ago.state.ne.us

Nevada
Bureau of Consumer Protection
Office of the Attorney General
100 N Carson Street
Carson City, NV 89701
775-684-1180
www.ag.state.nv.us

Nevada Consumer Affairs Division
1850 East Sahara Ave, Suite 101
Las Vegas, NV 89104
702-486-7355
Toll free: 800-326-5202 (NV)
TTY: 702-486-7901
Fax: 702-486-7371
E-mail: *NCAD@fyiconsumer.org*
www.fyiconsumer.org

Bureau of Consumer Protection
Attorney General's Office
555 E. Washington Ave., Suite 3900
Las Vegas, NV 89101
702-486-3420
Fax: 702-486-3768
www.ag.state.nv.us

Consumer Affairs Division
4600 Kietzke Lane, Building B, Suite 113
Reno, NV 89502
775-688-1800
Toll free: 800-326-5202 (NV)
TTY: 702-486-7901
Fax: 775-688-1803
E-mail: *renocad@fyiconsumer.org*
www.fyiconsumer.org

New Hampshire
Consumer Protection Bureau
Attorney General's Office
33 Capitol St.
Concord, NH 03301
603-271-3641
Toll free: 888-468-4454 (Consumer Protection Hotline)
TTY: 800-735-2964 (New Hampshire Only)
Fax: 603-223-6202
www.doj.nh.gov/consumer

New Jersey
Division of Consumer Affairs
Department of Law and Public Safety
PO Box 45027
Newark, NJ 07101
973-504-6200
Toll free: 800-242-5846 (NJ)
TTY: 973-504-6588
Fax: 973-648-3538
E-mail: *askconsumeraffairs@lps.state.nj.us*
www.njconsumeraffairs.gov

New Mexico
Consumer Protection Division
PO Drawer 1508
408 Galisteo Street
Santa Fe, NM 87501
505-827-6060
Toll free: 800-678-1508
Fax: 505-827-6685
www.nmag.gov

New York
Bureau of Consumer Frauds and Protection
Office of the Attorney General
State Capitol
Albany, NY 12224
518-474-5481
Toll free: 800-771-7755 (NY)
TTY: 800-788-9898 (Toll free)
Fax: 518-474-3618
www.oag.state.ny.us

New York State Consumer Protection Board
5 Empire State Plaza, Suite 2101
Albany, NY 12223-1556
518-474-8583 (Capitol Region)
Toll free: 800-697-1220
Fax: 518-474-2474
E-mail: *webmaster@consumer.state.ny.us*
www.nysconsumer.gov

Consumer Frauds and Protection Bureau
Office of the Attorney General
120 Broadway, 3rd Fl.
New York, NY 10271
212-416-8300
Toll free: 800-771-7755 (Hotline)
TTY: 800-788-9898 (Toll free) or 212-416-8893
Fax: 212-416-6003
www.oag.state.ny.us

North Carolina
Consumer Protection Division
Office of the Attorney General
9001 Mail Service Center
Raleigh, NC 27699-9001
919-716-6000
Toll free: 877-566-7226 (NC)
Fax: 919-716-6050
www.ncdoj.gov

North Dakota

Consumer Protection and Antitrust Division
Office of the Attorney General
600 E Boulevard Ave. Dept 125
Bismarck, ND 58505
701-328-3404
Toll free: 800-472-2600
TTY: 800-366-6888 (Toll free)
Fax: 701-328-5568
E-mail: *cpat@nd.gov*
www.ag.nd.gov

Ohio

Consumer Protection Section
Attorney General's Office
30 East Broad St., 14h Floor
Columbus, OH 43215-3428
614-466-4320
Toll free: 877-244-6446 (OH)
TTY: 614-466-1393
Fax: 614-728-7583
E-mail: *consumer@ag.state.oh.us*
www.ag.state.oh.us

Ohio Consumers' Counsel
10 W. Broad St. 18th Floor Suite 1800
Columbus, OH 43215
614-466-8574 (outside OH)
Toll free: 877-PICK-OCC (877-742-5622)
Fax: 614-466-9475
E-mail: *occ@occ.state.oh.us*
www.pickocc.org

Oklahoma

Oklahoma Department of Consumer Credit
4545 North Lincoln Blvd., #104
Oklahoma City, OK 73105
405-521-3653
Toll free: 800-448-4904
Fax: 405-521-6740
E-mail: *rbhooper@okdocc.state.ok.us*
www.okdocc.state.ok.us

Consumer Protection Unit
Oklahoma Attorney General
313 NE 21st Street
Oklahoma City, OK 73105
405-521-2029
Fax: 405-528-1867
www.oag.ok.gov

Oregon

Financial Fraud/Consumer Protection Section
Department of Justice
1162 Court St., NE
Salem, OR 97301
503-947-4333
503-378-4320 (Hotline Salem only)
503-229-5576 (Hotline Portland Only)
Toll free: 877-877-9392 (OR)
TTY: 503-378-5938
Fax: 503-378-5017
www.doj.state.or.us

Pennsylvania

Bureau of Consumer Protection
Office of Attorney General
16th Floor, Strawberry Square
Harrisburg, PA 17120
717-787-3391
Toll free: 800-441-2555 (PA)
Toll free: 877-888-4877 (PA—Health Care)
Toll free: 866-623-2137 (PA—Elder Abuse)
Fax: 717-787-8242
www.attorneygeneral.gov

Office of the Consumer Advocate
Office of the Attorney General
555 Walnut Street
5th Floor, Forum Place
Harrisburg, PA 17101-1923
717-783-5048 (Utilities only)
Toll free: 800-684-6560 (PA)
Fax: 717-783-7152
E-mail: *consumer@paoca.org*
www.oca.state.pa.us

Puerto Rico

Department de Asuntos Del Consumidor
Centro Gubernamental Roberto Sanchez Vilella
Edificio Norte
Apartado 41059, Estacion Minillas
San Juan, PR 00940-1059
787-722-7555
Fax: 787-726-0077
www.daco.gobierno.pr

Rhode Island

Consumer Protection Unit
Department of Attorney General
150 South Main St.
Providence, RI 02903
401-274-4400
TTY: 401-453-0410
Fax: 401-222-5110
www.riag.state.ri.us

South Carolina

South Carolina Department of Consumer Affairs
3600 Forest Drive, Suite 300
PO Box 5757
Columbia, SC 29250-5757
803-734-4200
Toll free: 800-922-1594 (SC)
TTY: 877-734-4215 (Toll free)
Fax: 803-734-4286
E-mail: *scdca@scconsumer.gov*
www.scconsumer.gov

Office of the Attorney General
PO Box 11549
Columbia, SC 29211-1549
803-734-3970
TTY: 803-734-4877
Fax: 803-253-6283
E-mail: *info@scattorneygeneral.com*
www.scattorneygeneral.org

South Dakota

Consumer Affairs
Office of the Attorney General
1302 E. Hwy 14, Suite 3
Pierre, SD 57501-8503
605-773-4400
Toll free: 800-300-1986 (SD)
TTY: 605-773-6585
Fax: 605-773-7163
E-mail: *consumerhelp@state.sd.us*
www.state.sd.us/atg

Tennessee

Division of Consumer Affairs
500 James Robertson Pkwy., 5th Floor
Nashville, TN 37243-0600
615-741-4737
Toll free: 800-342-8385 (TN)
Fax: 615-532-4994
E-mail: *consumer.affairs@state.tn.us*
www.tn.gov/consumer

Consumer Advocate and Protection Division
Office of the Attorney General
PO Box 20207
Nashville, TN 37202-0207
615-741-1671
Fax: 615-532-2910
www.attorneygeneral.state.tn.us

Texas

Regional Offices
Austin Regional Office
PO Box 12548
Austin, TX 78711-2548
512-463-2100
Toll free: 800-621-0508
Fax: 512-473-8301
www.oag.state.tx.us

Dallas Regional Office
Office of the Attorney General
1412 Main Street, Suite 810
Dallas, TX 75202
214-969-5310
Fax: 214-969-7615
www.oag.state.tx.us

El Paso Regional Office
Office of the Attorney General
401 East Franklin Ave., Suite 530
El Paso, TX 79901
915-834-5800
Fax: 915-542-1546
E-mail: *public.information@oag.state.tx.us*
www.oag.state.tx.us

Houston Regional Office—Consumer Protection
Office of the Attorney General
808 Travis, Suite 300
Houston, TX 77002-1702
713-223-5886
Toll free: 800-252-8011 (TX)
Fax: 713-223-5821
www.oag.state.tx.us

Lubbock Regional Office
Office of the Attorney General
4630 50th Street, Suite 500
Lubbock, TX 79414-3520
806-747-5238
Fax: 806-747-6307
www.oag.state.tx.us

McAllen Regional Office
Office of the Attorney General
3201 North McColl Road, Suite B
McAllen, TX 78501-1685
956-682-4547
Toll free: 800-252-8011 (TX)
Fax: 956-682-1957
www.oag.state.tx.us

San Antonio Regional Office
Office of the Attorney General
115 East Travis St., Suite 925
San Antonio, TX 78205-1605
210-224-1007
Toll free: 800-252-8011 (TX)
Fax: 210-225-1075
www.oag.state.tx.us

Utah

Division of Consumer Protection
Department of Commerce
160 East 300 South
PO Box 146704
Salt Lake City, UT 84114-6704
801-530-6601
Fax: 801-530-6001
E-mail: *consumerprotection@utah.gov*
www.consumerprotection.utah.gov

Vermont

Consumer Assistance Program
Office of the Attorney General
104 Morrill Hall, UVM
Burlington, VT 05405
802-656-3183
Toll free: 800-649-2424 (VT)
Fax: 802-656-1423
E-mail: *consumercomplaint@atg.state.vt.us*
www.atg.state.vt.us

Vermont Agency of Agriculture, Food, and Markets
Food Safety and Consumer Protection
Consumer Protection
116 State Street
Montpelier, VT 05620-2901
802-828-2436
Fax: 802-828-5983
E-mail: *carolyn.moulton@state.vt.us*
www.vermontagriculture.com

Virgin Islands

Virgin Islands Offices
Department of Licensing and Consumer Affairs
3000 Golden Rock Shopping Center, Suite 9
Christiansted, VI 00820-4311
340-773-2226
www.dlca.gov.vi

Virginia
State Offices
Antitrust and Consumer Litigation Section
Office of the Attorney General
900 East Main St.
Richmond, VA 23219
804-786-2116
Toll free: 800-451-1525
Fax: 804-786-0122
E-mail: *mail@oag.state.va.us*
www.oag.state.va.us

Office of Consumer Affairs
Department of Agriculture and Consumer Services
Oliver W. Hill Building
102 Governor Street
Richmond, VA 23219
804-786-2042
Toll free: 800-552-9963 (VA)
TTY: 800-828-1120 (Toll free)
Fax: 804-225-2666
www.vdacs.virginia.gov

Washington
State Offices
Office of the Attorney General
800 Fifth Avenue, Ste. 2000
Seattle, WA 98104
Toll free: 800-551-4636
www.atg.wa.gov

West Virginia
State Offices
Consumer Protection Division
Office of the Attorney General
812 Quarrier St., 1st Floor
PO Box 1789
Charleston, WV 25326-1789
304-558-8986
Toll free: 800-368-8808 (WV)
Fax: 304-558-0184
E-mail: *consumer@wvago.gov*
www.wvago.gov

Wisconsin
State Offices
Department of Agriculture, Trade and Consumer Protection
2811 Agriculture Dr.
PO Box 8911
Madison, WI 53708-8911
608-224-4976
Toll free: 800-422-7128 (WI)
TTY: 608-224-5058
Fax: 608-224-4939
E-mail: *datcphotline@wi.gov*
www.datcp.state.wi.us

Wyoming
State Offices
Consumer Protection Unit
Office of the Attorney General
2424 Pioneer Avenue, 1st Floor
Cheyenne, WY 82002
307-777-7841
Toll free: 800-438-5799
Fax: 307-777-7956
E-mail: *agwebmaster@state.wy.us*
http://attorneygeneral.state.wy.us

FURTHER READING

Abagnale, Frank W. *Stealing Your Life: The Ultimate Identity Theft Prevention Plan.* Broadway, 2007

Atlantic Publishing Company. *The Online Identity Theft Prevention Kit: Stop Scammers, Hackers, and Identity Thieves from Ruining Your Life.* Atlantic Publishing Company, 2008

Bidwell, Teri. *Hack Proofing Your Identity.* Syngress, 2002

Carter, T. *Insider's Secrets To Identity Theft: What They Don't Want You to Know.* LuLu, 2006

Collins, Judith. *Investigating Identity Theft: A Guide for Businesses, Law Enforcement, and Victims.* Wiley, 2006

Cullen, Terri. *The Complete Identity Theft Guidebook: How to Protect Yourself from the Most Pervasive Crime in America.* Three Rivers Press, 2007

Hammond Jr., Robert. *Identity Theft: How to Protect Your Most Valuable Asset.* Career Press, 2003

Hastings, Glenn and Marcus, Richard. *Identity Theft, Inc.: A Wild Ride with the World's #1 Identity Thief.* The Disinformation Company, 2006

Lininger, Rachael and Vines, Russell Dean. *Phishing: Cutting the Identity Theft Line;* Wiley (May 6, 2005)

Luna, J.J. *How to Be Invisible: The Essential Guide to Protecting Your Personal Privacy, Your Assets, and Your Life* (Revised Edition). Thomas Dunne Books, 2004

Savelli, Lou. *Pocket Guide to Identity Theft.* Looseleaf Law Publications, 2004

Sullivan, Bob. *Your Evil Twin: Behind the Identity Theft Epidemic.* Wiley, 2004

Weisman, Steve. *50 Ways to Protect Your Identity and Your Credit: Everything You Need to Know about Identity Theft, Credit Cards, Credit Repair, and Credit Reports.* Prentice Hall, 2005

ACKNOWLEDGMENTS

My lovely wife Tara has been very supportive throughout the writing of this book, as have my wonderful children Lauren, Samara, Ben, Alex, and Becca. My knowledgeable stepchildren Gordon, James, and Pat have always been willing to talk to me about what I write and I appreciate their encouragement. Thanks to my super agent Grace Freedson, who keeps finding me work, and to my good friend Jim Carr, who is always willing to read and critique what I write.

INDEX

ABOUT THE AUTHOR

DAVID H. HOLTZMAN is an Internet pioneer who helped oversee the commercial Internet's wild growth in the turbulent mid-1990s. He is also the author of *Privacy Lost: How Technology Is Endangering Your Privacy* (Jossey-Bass, 2006). He has been interviewed by major news media including the *New York Times*, CNN, and *USA Today*. Holtzman wrote a monthly ethics and privacy column called "Flashpoint" for *CSO* [Chief Security Officer] *Magazine,* and his essays on privacy and security have been published in *BusinessWeek*, *Wired* magazine, CNET, and ZDNet.

During the dot-com boom, Holtzman ran the critical infrastructure of the Internet—the domain name system. As chief technology officer of Network Solutions and the manager of the Internet's master root server, Holtzman oversaw the growth of the Internet from 500,000 to over 20,000,000 domain names.

A former cryptographic analyst, Russian linguist, and submariner with the U.S. Naval Security Group, Holtzman has worked at the Defense Special Missile and Astronautics Center as an intelligence analyst, focusing chiefly on the Soviet manned space program.

He has consulted on marketing strategy for several large corporations and served as Chief Technology Officer of Senator Bayh's All America PAC, as well as a security advisor to General Wesley Clark's presidential campaign in 2004.

He has served on the boards of several privately held companies in the United States, Canada, and Singapore, as well as nonprofit organizations and universities. He is on the Board of Visitors of the School of Information Sciences at the University of Pittsburgh. He has been an advisor to over a dozen high-tech companies in Washington, D.C., Silicon Valley, Austin, Canada, and New York. He has taught courses as an adjunct MBA professor at American University in Washington, D.C., and entrepreneurship at the University of Pittsburgh, innovating a cutting-edge "Lecture On Demand" technique using podcasting.

Holtzman holds a BS in Computer Science from the University of Maryland and a BA in Philosophy from the University of Pittsburgh, as well as being an honors graduate in Russian from the Defense Language Institute.

Holtzman is the father of five children and has three grandchildren, three stepchildren, and two children-in-law. When not at home in Herndon, Virginia, Holtzman lives part of the year on Prince Edward Island in Canada with his wonderful wife, Tara. He likes to sail, cook, snowmobile, watch classical theater, and listen to jazz and blues.

Holtzman occasionally blogs at *www.globalpov.com* and can be reached at *david@globalpov.com*.